L

the Recycled Nun

Barbara Richmond

Printed in the United States of America
International Standard Book Number: 1-883928-25-7
Library of Congress Catalog Card Number: 97-069956

Published by:
Longwood Communications
397 Kingslake Drive
DeBary, FL 32713
904-774-1991

Dedication

To my husband, Mike, whose wholehearted commitment to the Lord and daily example of the life of faith has been the greatest visible influence on the "recycling" of my life.

Acknowledgments

My deepest appreciation to my husband and my children for their constant encouragement, prayers and patience during the time I wrote this book.

I am also very grateful to those friends who read the manuscript and gave helpful suggestions, as well as to the faithful supporters of this ministry who by their prayers and practical assistance continually stand with me as I seek to fulfill the call of God on my life.

To all who read the first edition of *Recycled Nun* and who urged me to expand and re-publish it in its present form, I thank you. Your enthusiasm regarding this testimony and your desire to see it in the hands of many more people is deeply appreciated.

Last, special thanks are due to Pastor Jack Hayford of Church on the Way, Van Nuys, California, whose persuasive exhortation to me to write this book got me started.

Contents

Introduction

I suppose that books can be written for many different reasons, some laudable, some not. As a Christian, a wife, a mother, and a woman in full-time ministry, it has been my desire to write this book for the following specific purposes:

1. To bring glory to God. "For all things are for your sakes, that the grace which is spreading to more and more people may cause the giving of thanks to abound to the glory of God" (2 Corinthians 4:15).

2. To testify of the marvelous grace and love of our Lord Jesus Christ, as evidenced by His working in my life. "But in all these things we overwhelmingly conquer

through Him who loved us" (Romans 8:37).

3. To edify my fellow believers. "And let us consider how to stimulate one another to love and good deeds … encouraging one another; and all the more, as you see the day drawing near" (Hebrews 10:24-25).

4. To share the Good News that God's love through Jesus is available today, to whosoever will call upon the Lord. "Jesus Christ is the same yesterday and today, yes and forever" (Hebrews 13:8). "That if you confess with your mouth Jesus as Lord, and believe in your heart that God raised Him from the dead, you shall be saved; for with the heart man believes, resulting in righteousness, and with the mouth he confesses, resulting in salvation" (Romans 10:9-10).

It is my fervent prayer that the reading of this book will be for you one of those experiences in which "the eyes of your heart may be enlightened, so that you may know what is the hope of His calling, what are the riches of the glory of His inheritance in the saints, and what is the surpassing greatness of His power toward us who believe" (Ephesians 1:18-19).

What He's done for me, He can do for you!

I

BEHIND THOSE CONVENT WALLS

Silence descended like a great shroud over the long dormitories and dark corridors of the Convent of the Holy Names that July night in 1962. It was hot on the second floor and too light a breeze from the open window gently moved the stark white curtains dividing alcove from alcove. As the last tinkling sounds of the Grand Silence bell died away, hushed breathing and a few stifled sobs were all that could be hard in the blackness. Eighteen new recruits to this convent life — tired, a bit homesick, and a bit awed by their new surroundings — longed for a good night's rest and yet drove sleep away with the racing thoughts of their stimulated minds. For many it seemed to be the longest day of their lives, this second of July. Fresh from a round of high school proms, graduation parties, and high school fun, they were suddenly thrust into a world apart. What awaited them was clouded in their imaginations, and it was with a mixture of fear and hope, joy and anxiety, that most had taken the step from the comfort of home and family to the strange and mysterious world of cloistered life.

I lay there that night, one of those new postulants, as we were called, happy, yet torn with mixed emotions. Yes, I was happy to be here. I'd dreamed about it so long — this place where I was sure I could be holy and close to God, where I could serve other people; this place from which I might someday be sent overseas for missionary service. I really thought I might like that, and I found it exciting to think God might choose me for that kind of service.

I was also frightened as I lay there in that little bed. I was 250 miles away from home. It might as well have been 250,000; I'd never been that far away before. But it was more than the miles. I was far, far away from everything familiar and comfortable, everything known and treasured. I was more homesick than I cared to admit to myself. I thought about my mother and blinked back a tear. When I left her two days before, she'd been crying, assuring me she wanted me to go, but that she would miss me. My dad was very quiet; he never said much, but I knew that deep down in his heart he wasn't thrilled with what I was doing. He would have loved nothing more than a houseful of grandchildren, but those hopes were dashed when I donned the black veil. I was an only child, and when I entered the convent, my dad gave up more than I did.

I heard some muffled tears to my left and knew they must be Janet's. She seemed to be having an especially hard time earlier in the day. I wondered what brought her here and if she had some of the same feelings I did. She was so pretty when I first saw her coming through the door. Tall, dark-haired, and beautifully dressed, she looked much older than her eighteen years. She had flashed me an uncertain smile and then she was gone. Sometime later she joined the rest of us in the recreation room, now attired in her postulant's garb — a long black dress, white collar, black stockings and shoes. The change was startling. With the makeup washed off, her beautiful long hair pulled back unceremoniously, how young and yes, how frightened she looked. Something about her made me like her, and now she was crying. I prayed a minute for her and hoped she would be comforted. With a weary sigh, I rolled over and tried to sleep. It would be a long day tomorrow.

Five thirty in the morning is unbelievably early! I was sure I must be dreaming, but unfortunately I wasn't. There she was, all dressed and smiling, waking me for prayer time. Putting a finger to her lips to remind me that the Grand Silence was still in effect and that I should get ready noiselessly, she motioned to me to meet her at the doorway of the dormitory in five minutes. *Five minutes!* I thought. It will take me longer than that just to figure out how these clothes go on!

Sister Alice Elizabeth, my "angel," was a year my senior in the religious life, and she, along with the other novices, had been assigned to help the fledglings adapt for the first few days. She took me through the morning routine as though she'd always lived here, and as I followed her with some confusion, I wondered if I'd ever be as efficient.

That first day was much easier than any of us had expected. To honor the newcomers, conversation was permitted in the dining room during meals. We all thought that there was nothing unusual about talking while we ate until a few days later when the mealtime became very quiet. We quickly learned that silence was the norm during meals.

We celebrated the Fourth of July with games and an outdoor picnic, played volleyball with great enthusiasm, took vigorous walks in the woods around the convent, and ran races up and down the hills—skirts and veils flying in the wind like parachutes and laughter ringing through the trees — for five days.

Then the bomb fell.

Now that we were somewhat acclimated to our new residence, much of the fun and games had to go. Mother Mistress, the Superior directly responsible for the training of new recruits, was a charming, delightful, motherly woman, very obviously in love with the God she served. She could not have been more perfectly suited for this position. She was every bit a "mother" and, I dare say, more of a mother to some than the ones they left at home. Her infectious laughter, her kind and gentle ways, and that ever present smile, endeared her to us from the first day. But she could also be serious, and rightly so, for she was totally committed to living a dedicated life and to fostering the same unwavering dedication and faithfulness in those under her charge.

She brought us together for our first training meeting, and with all the seriousness and gentleness at her command, began to instruct us in some of the basic principles by which we must henceforth live. Convent life would be happy, she explained, in the measure that we submitted to and obeyed the Holy Rule, which we would memorize. The Superior, any Superior in authority over us at a given time, was to be to us the voice of God. Her directives were His, her commands His will, to be obeyed instantly, cheerfully, and without question. Acts of penance were to be a part of our regular routine. Discipline of self, sacrifice, prayer, meditation, and an attitude of a servant must all be integrated in our lives to the point that each element flowed with the others in one expression of commitment to God. To help us in our self-denial, there would be specific deeds of penance required of us on a weekly basis.

The longer she spoke, the more nervous I became. I could feel tension in the air around me. Her cautious manner warned us that something was coming. As she continued, my heart was in my throat.

Mother Mistress hesitated as if groping for the best words. It was time, she continued, that we learn the Acts of Penance so that we could begin practicing them every week. She proceeded to explain. At a time of our choosing during the week, we would eat a meal on our knees instead of seated at a table. Upon entering the dining room, instead of going to our assigned place, we were to kneel in front of the head table, wait until grace was said and the sisters were all seated, and then beg for our meal from the presiding Superior.

At another time during the week, we would follow the same procedure of kneeling in the front, but instead of begging for our food, we were to publicly accuse ourselves before the assembled community of an infraction of the rule and ask the community's forgiveness. Such infractions might be: "I accuse myself of being distracted in the chapel," or "I accuse myself of speaking during silence," or "I accuse myself of looking around in the dining room and failing to keep my eyes cast down." She continued with several other examples and concluded by saying that we must kneel there until the Superior gave us penance to perform in atonement for our failings and excused to our place. The penance would usually be a specific prayer to repeat.

I felt the color rising in my cheeks.

There was more. Once a week, we would participate in the Chapter of Faults in the community room. The entire household would be assembled, with the Superior seated at one end and the sisters seated in several long rows down each side of the room, chairs facing each other with a wide aisle left open in the center. By turns, beginning with the youngest and ending with the oldest, each sister would rise, walk to the center front, kneel before the Superior, accuse herself of some infraction, and then wait in silence while any of the other sisters were free also to accuse the kneeling figure of offenses they alleged she had committed in the past week. It was very clear; the issue was not whether their allegations were true. At stake in this exercise was growth in humility.

As each sister was accused by the others, she would be scrutinized very closely by Mother Superior. Every reaction on her face would be noted until she could successfully arrive at the pinnacle of what the Rule called humility: that is, to kneel and be accused of anything, no matter how bizarre, without reacting with the least bit of emotion. One was considered truly holy and Christlike if "all manner of evil could be said" while one knelt there motionless, "as a lamb to the slaughter."

Mother Mistress assured us that new postulants generally found this to be the hardest of the penances and that we would not be expected to master our pride immediately. That she should see progress as the weeks passed was all that was essential at this point.

My flushed face was now bright red.

The rest of what she said blurred in my mind as I tried to grasp the impact of these penitential practices. They were the first real test of how deep my desire was to serve God and to give Him anything He asked for, but had I not come here after all to find that close and special relationship with Jesus Christ? And didn't I know that it would mean things like this? I'd been reading all the books since grammar school. I knew how all those saints who "made it" in the church had all engaged in strict disciplinary practices, fasted, prayed long hours and slept little. Somehow in their biographies it had seemed a whole lot more spiritual than it sounded to me right now, sitting in that community room, pondering the weight of a Chapter of Faults!

The sound of shuffling feet brought me out of my distractions as sisters quickly stood to their feet when Mother Mistress arose. Nervously I looked around, realizing I had missed the last instructions and I didn't know what we were to do next. Conformity saved me as I fell into line with the other postulants and was able to deduce that we had some free time, silent free time, as the line made its way down the long hall to the dormitory and postulants began disappearing behind white curtains.

I threw myself on my bed, face down, and tried to pray. Only one thought crossed my mind again and again: *God, help me not to fail You now.* I reexamined my motives and my purpose for coming to this place less than a week ago. (Could it really be just five days?) I had thought that most of the cost of religious life was paid in the days surrounding my entrance: leaving home, family, friends; abandoning hopes for a different future. I began to understand that those things were just a small down payment; now that the real cost was beginning to be felt, I had to reckon with the fact that, like a long-term mortgage, I would be paying for the rest of my life.

I knew that this was just the first of many such instructional meetings; that if these requirements had been placed on us when the fragrance of abandoned pleasures still lingered in the air around us, there must be sterner things ahead. I had already heard that being a postulant was child's play compared to the two years' training as a novice. I shuddered and wondered what else was hidden in the pages of that fearful little black book, reverentially called the Holy Rule.

I slid off my bed and dropped to my knees on the hard floor. I renewed my commitment to serve God, no matter what the cost. I told Him again that I loved Him and that I wanted to be all that He expected me to be. I prayed for grace, for strength, for stamina, and for perseverance. One thing I knew—I wanted to go to heaven, and I wanted to be close to Him. I was convinced that nothing else in life was as important as that. I believed that being a nun was the quickest way to fulfill that goal, and I was dedicated to being not just a nun, but the best nun I could be.

As July stretched into August, my resolve grew, and each day found me more determined and motivated to work my way to sainthood — and quickly! I decided that if it was good to be holy, it was better to be holy quickly, so I was off and running on my private spiritual marathon.

It would be several years before I learned that as good as desire may be, it is not enough; works will never do it, and that what I sought *could* be found, but in ways far from where I was.

II

Whose Baby Shall This Be?

The sun was not quite over the horizon, but already it was unseasonably warm for late April. The world was at war and weary, wondering how much longer men and boys would continue to die in Europe and in the Pacific. The year was 1945, and thousands of families mourned soldiers lost in the almost three and a half years since Pearl Harbor.

But thoughts of war were not uppermost in the minds of three who carefully and quickly drove through the streets of Fall River, Massachusetts, in the early dawn of April 20th. "Hurry, Daddy, hurry!" cried young Norma Cleaves from the back seat of the car as they sped toward the hospital.

Breathlessly abandoning his car and his wife at the emergency entrance, Mr. Cleaves rushed his young daughter into the arms of the first nurse he saw, urging her to take Norma up quickly lest the baby be born in the hallway!

With swift efficiency, an attendant whisked young Norma into a wheelchair and into the nearest elevator. Upstairs, nurses and doctors hastened their preparations, for it was obvious that the child about to be born would not wait. Gowns were donned, face masks secured, the young mother prepared; before the new grandparents had arrived in the second floor waiting room, a healthy eight-pound baby girl made her entrance into this world with a hearty cry. A nurse standing by the new mother's head bent down to wipe the damp forehead and was first to notice the tear-filled eyes. "Is this your first…?" she began, but stopped as the young woman on the table broke into heart-rending sobs. "I can't keep her, I can't keep her! Don't let me see her or I won't be able to stand it."

She sobbed as though she would never stop, and the nurse cried quietly with her. The baby was quickly removed to the nursery where a gentle, white-clad figure attended to her needs, holding her just a little longer than usual as if to comfort the crying infant, so quickly deprived of mother and family.

Sometime later that day, out of the recovery room and settled in her bed at the far end of the hall where she couldn't hear the cries of the newborns, a very troubled and heartbroken young mother named the baby she would never see and filled out the preliminary forms for placing the little girl for adoption. Her parents looked on with mixed emotions as she answered the social worker's questions.

Norma was her daddy's favorite. They could talk about anything and everything, and it was always to him that she went when trouble came. Some months earlier when she realized she was pregnant, she had panicked at the prospect of telling her mother, knowing the wrath that was sure to ensue. So Norma had sought out Daddy. As she told him the news, he listened as he always did — with his heart. In his characteristic manner, his blue eyes met hers as with a calm voice as he said, "You love well, my daughter, but not wisely. Norma, Norma, how shall we tell your mother?"

Norma knew what that meant: "How will *I* tell your mother?" He would protect this dearly loved daughter; he always did.

Now as the social worker collected the various papers Norma had signed, the young mother looked at her father and said simply, "I named her Barbara. I hope she gets to keep the name, but I'll never know. God, I just hope she has a good home."

She covered her face with her hands, and Mr. Cleaves motioned to his wife to come aside. Once more he asked her to please relent, but she was adamant. Norma *must* give up the baby. There was no way to provide for it. Didn't they already have their hands full with two-year-old Judy, sick all the time and requiring so much time, attention and expensive medical help? Shouldn't they have insisted that Norma place Judy for adoption two years before when she gave birth to her in this very same hospital? Perhaps this second pregnancy might never have occurred if Norma had experienced the pain of surrendering her first child to unknown parents. No, it was not possible. There was no alternative. The baby deserved a better home, and Norma deserved to feel the consequences of her actions. Mr. Cleaves turned from his wife with a heavy heart and a deep sigh.

Two days later, Norma Cleaves left the hospital and her baby daughter who would be cared for and raised by strangers. It was worse than death, and the pain wrenched her heart. She went home to Judy to cry and wonder whether her new baby would grow to resemble this curly-haired toddler.

As the weeks passed, Norma determined to put the grief out of her thoughts as much as possible. What could not be changed must be accepted, and so she disciplined herself to forget about baby Barbara, though she never fully could. Christmas and birthdays were to become the hardest times. As Norma wrapped and hid gifts for Judy, she would wonder about her other little girl. And when Daddy celebrated his birthday and Norma did something special for him, her heart would ache as her mind would go back to that birthday when Daddy had turned fifty, the day that little Barbara had been born. Where was she? Was anyone giving her a birthday party? Did she have a good home? So many questions would invade her thoughts, and Norma would again have to push the memories away.

Meanwhile, less that twenty-five miles away in Taunton, a young couple unable to have children of their own prayed and waited, waited and prayed for a baby. They had contacted an agency and in due time had been promised a son. They had seen him, held him, and eagerly anticipated his arrival. Then at the last moment the natural mother had changed her mind, and Manuel and Izaura Pires were without their baby boy. It had been a keen disappointment. But now a little girl was available.

Izaura, better known as Hazel, nervously dialed long distance to her mother and sisters twenty miles away in New Bedford. Her voice shook a little as she relayed the news. This very day the baby would come! Excited squeals at the other end of the line made her even more nervous. The lingering thought plagued her, *What if this child should be recalled*? It was a very real fear.

More agitated than an expectant father in a hospital waiting room, Manuel paced back and forth, wearing a path in the rug while waiting for the car carrying their precious bundle. As he peered out the window for what seemed to be the thousandth time, a black sedan pulled up out front.

Unwrapping a faded pink blanket, Manuel and Izaura took their first look at the new daughter. She had honey-colored hair, big dark eyes, and a round face that reminded her new daddy of a pumpkin. That promptly became her "name of endearment."

Yes, she was cute, but oh, how she cried!

After her birth, Barbara had been cared for in several foster homes over the months and on this day had been removed from a family who had grown to love her and had planned to adopt her. Responding as infants do to a loving environment, the baby was as attached to them as they were to her. Suddenly over some legal technicality, the child had been taken from the home with both mother and baby nearly hysterical. The priest who delivered the crying infant to the Pires had been unable to comfort her and suspected she was fearful of strangers. He was also sure that the traumatic departure earlier in the day was still affecting the child. Assuring Manuel she would be fine in a little while and mumbling something about other families who were awaiting his arrival, he left.

So went my introduction to the parents who raised me and provided for me for the next seventeen years. All night long I cried. First my mother, then my father, walked the floor with a child who would not be comforted. I would not eat; I would not sleep; I would not lie in the crib. Who but the Lord knows what was going through my heart and mind that first night in the home that would become my own.

For three days my parents had no rest. On the weekend, doting aunts and an excited first-time grandmother came by train from New Bedford to see the new addition. Aunt Lean, relieving my exhausted mother for a while, picked me up and walked and talked to me until I finally stopped crying and fell into a fitful sleep, to everyone's great relief.

The story of my arrival has been told and retold through the years, and I have sometimes wondered at the stamina of my parents. It is to their credit that they endured a crying, sometimes screaming baby for three days without giving up on me! They learned to love me as their own, for I really was their dream come true!

My dad, a hard-working factory machine operator, immigrated from the Azores Islands of Portugal at the age of sixteen. He crossed the Atlantic with his fourteen-year-old brother in a less than adequate boat to seek a better life in the United States. He worked diligently, married young, and owned his first home by the time he was nineteen. His wife was devoted to him. They had a son who died at birth. The young mother never recovered physically nor from her sorrow, and over the next few months one complication after another robbed her of her health. Barely into her thirties, she died.

Lonely and still young himself, my dad was introduced about a year later to the Airozo family of New Bedford, also Azorean immigrants. He began to court the youngest daughter, Izaura, and in November 1939 they were married in her church in New Bedford. Having never traveled outside her hometown, the twenty-mile move to Taunton was indeed a big step for the happy bride. The newlyweds adjusted nicely to each other and life was happy, but for one recurring disappointment: Hazel, as Izaura was called, did not become pregnant.

Now with my arrival in the home some six years after the marriage, that cloud over their relationship was removed. While they waited out the tense months until the adoption could be finalized in court, my parents busied themselves with making a good home for me.

Back in Fall River, Judy, my half-sister, was growing up under the watchful eye of her grandparents and her mother, who was busy working long hours to provide in the place of the father who was not there. Months passed, and when the time came for that final, irrevocable surrender of her second daughter, Norma signed her name with a firm hand, relinquishing all rights to her child and all hopes of future relationship, promising to refrain from any attempt at a reunion. As the original birth certificate was torn and burned as if to eradicate the fact that Barbara Cleaves ever existed, Norma resigned herself to the fact that not only was this chapter in her life now closed, but even more, it could never be reopened.

And so it was...at least for the next thirty years.

III

Portuguese Catholic in 1950s America

My dad loved the city of Taunton, the town he'd come to many years before as a teenager, and my mother grew to like it as her own hometown. We would probably have stayed there permanently except for an unfortunate turn of events when I was four.

The factory where my dad worked went out of business, and jobs were hard to come by, especially for a man over forty years of age, which my dad now was. For several weeks my parents worried and searched out new avenues of employment. When a job finally became available in a New Bedford factory similar to the one where he had worked in Taunton, there seemed to be no choice but to move.

Initially, my dad would leave home Sunday night on the train, live with my grandmother for the week, and return to us Friday evening. After a few months of this lonely lifestyle, he began to look for an apartment. My grandmother, eager to have her only grandchild nearby, must have suggested in many ways during those first weeks that New Bedford was really a very nice place to live. So, in a short while we settled into a third floor tenement dwelling just minutes away from my grandmother and aunts.

It was very difficult for my dad to leave Taunton with all its memories and friends, but he was always conscientious when it came to his family. He had inherited a strong sense of duty from his parents, who had raised thirteen children in a three-room house on the island of Terceira. They didn't have much by today's standards, but there was always food on the table and concern for one another. When it came to his family, my dad would always do whatever had to be done to see that we were taken care of, regardless of how he felt.

From the age of four, my home was New Bedford, Massachusetts, with its long streets lined with three-story tenement houses, postage-stamp-sized yards, and miles of factories along the waterfront. The bulk of the population was of Portuguese descent; many were recent immigrants with more arriving every year, fleeing islands whose stubborn soil would not grow enough food and whose dangerous seas refused to yield enough fish to feed a growing population. They came looking for a land of promise and riches, and many were keenly disappointed.

Long hours in hot, smelly factories had not figured in their dreams of the great America. Winters colder than anything they had ever known threatened to paralyze their hopes, but the Portuguese are not easily discouraged.

Despite the hardships of life in America, it also gave them a hope that was unavailable back on the islands. Here hardship walked hand in hand with hope and promise that hard work would yield satisfactory results. Back in the old country, hardship walked a lonely road that ended only in death. So these immigrants continually encouraged relatives back on the islands to come and join them.

In this environment I grew up learning Portuguese as my first language and embracing old world traditions which were part and parcel of new world living. We were devout Catholics whose lives pretty much centered around home and church. My grandmother went to Mass every day and prayed her rosary continually. I would often stay with her, and inevitably she had stories to tell me of this or that saint, stories often so shrouded in tradition that it was difficult to separate fact from fiction.

My mother was determined that I would have a Catholic education, and as school age approached, my parents faced a difficult decision.

New Bedford, though not a large city by general standards, boasted thirty-two Catholic churches, many more than actually needed to serve the population. National feeling was strong so there were several Portuguese Catholic churches, some French, some Irish, two Polish, an Italian, a Lebanese, a German, and others. The membership of each parish was very dedicated not only to the church but also to its national heritage. Sermons were preached in the native tongue of the communicants, and Catholics were very segregated by cultural and national traditions, though they all pledged allegiance to Rome. It was unthinkable that a Polish family should join the German parish, though they lived right next door to it and the Polish church was located across town.

Therefore, when my parents opted for membership in

the nearby Irish parish which operated an elementary school instead of the Portuguese parish without a school, it was a radical departure from tradition in a fiercely traditional town. With membership came the guarantee that I would be received into the school. So, shortly after we arrived in New Bedford, I entered kindergarten at the age of almost four and a half, speaking fluent Portuguese in a classroom full of English-speaking youngsters.

From the first day I had two strikes against me; one I quickly overcame, and the other was a source of recurring problems through the years. Learning English posed little difficulty with daily exposure to an abundantly crowded classroom of talkative five-year-olds. Catholic schools in the '50s were known for the large classes, and the sisters thought nothing of handling classes upwards of forty and fifty squirming youngsters. However, the age difference between me and my classmates was not so easily dismissed. Periodically, at critical transitional stages of growth and development, the fact that I was a year younger than my companions separated me socially and emotionally from them and gave birth to assorted difficulties.

Generally I liked school and school liked me. Books became my best friends as I mastered the art of reading. As early as second grade, I remember wanting to be a writer and would sit by the hour writing stories and poems.

That was a special year, second grade. From the earliest days in September, Sister Mary Peter diligently taught and trained us in preparation for that great event in a seven-year-old Catholic child's life—First Communion. From the Baltimore catechism we memorized all the right answers. even mastering the word *Transubstantiation,* though we were hard pressed to understand what it meant. What we did understand was that Jesus would come to us in a unique way and reside in our hearts for exactly fifteen minutes! We were to prepare ourselves very carefully and make a list of all the things we especially wanted to ask Him, because everybody knew that God answered all of a child's prayers on his or her First Communion day.

The Mass and all its implications of Jesus dying over and over again symbolically to atone for our sins was explained on our second grade level, and our instructions built up to the point that when the time came for my first venture into the confessional box to tell all my horrible sins to the priest, I couldn't wait to rid myself of the load of guilt I felt for being the cause of the death of Jesus again and again. I wondered how I could last a whole week without going to confession. I was so sure that I would fail somehow and be miserable until the following Saturday's confession time.

All of us in the First Communion class were taken in a group for our first confession, and for the rest of the day I lived as if paralyzed, so petrified was I that I would sin and make myself unworthy to receive communion the following morning. I even asked to go to bed early that night, wanting to spend as much time as possible asleep, concluding that as long as I was sleeping I would be incapable of sinning.

Sister Mary Peter had indoctrinated us successfully. The need to be absolutely pure of soul to be worthy to receive Jesus in Holy Communion had been deeply impressed on my young mind. I actually remember praying that night that God would let me die immediately after my First Communion because I was so terrified with the enormity of the task ahead: purity of soul, freedom from sin, sufficient good works to be made acceptable for heaven. Catholic doctrine teaches that children up to the age of seven, the age of reason as laid down by Canon Law, are taken to heaven if they die because they are not old enough to be accountable. Living to my eighth birthday seemed a fate worse than death, and I *literally* trembled under the load of fear.

Tucked into bed, bathed, hair carefully wound in rag curlers — with the spotless white dress and veil laid out for the following morning — I turned my thoughts to the list of requests I should have ready for Jesus when He came to me the next day.

I don't remember when it was that my parents first explained to me that I was adopted and what this meant, but it was sometime before this momentous occasion. Sister Mary Peter had said that all of our prayers would be answered. I was sure that she knew everything about God and was always right. To our young minds the sisters couldn't make mistakes!

I did not hesitate to formulate my petitions. It was a short list and I remember it clearly:

Dear Jesus,

1. Please let me find my real mother.

2. Please give me brothers and sisters.

Amen.

That was all. Barely past my seventh birthday, I already had a strong conviction that some day, some way, I would find the mother who had given me life. I was utterly convinced that she gave me up because she was unable to care for me. If even the hint of an implication was ever made that I was not wanted by her, I was furious. Other mothers might not want their children, but *not* my mother. She wanted me; I knew she did. She just didn't have enough money to feed me. That's what I'd been told by my adoptive parents who put the best construction on the situation that they could. Since they spoke well of the young woman they never knew, but who had been the vehicle for the answer to their prayers, I really believed what they told me of her, little as it was. Many years would pass before I would finally learn whether or not I was right.

My education continued in St. Kilian's elementary school. My report cards were consistently good, which delighted my parents to whom a good education was of paramount importance. I liked most of the nuns and embraced all of their religious teaching.

A few memories of those years stand out.

In the third grade I learned for the first time that all those other people, "Protestants" they were called, were going to hell and that I should thank God every day that I was born Catholic. We were heartily exhorted to stay with "our own" lest we be tainted by the devil's heresies which the Protestants believed. We heard long and eloquent teachings in our religion class about that terrible priest, Martin Luther, who left the church and married a nun. All those poor Protestants since then were going to be condemned because of that one man.

In fourth grade I discovered that nuns could cry. Our teacher that year was sick but still responsible for a classroom of fifty ten-year-olds. There were times when the poor woman was distraught with trying to handle the boys and would break down in tears before the class, pleading with them to behave since she was too sick to discipline them. The boys would laugh; I would feel sick inside. I wasn't surprised when she died not too long after the end of that school year. Only God knows what that poor woman went through. I have thought of her from time to time, and sincerely hoped she knew the Lord's saving grace.

By the time I was ten, my spiritual life was developing according to sound Catholic tradition. Every night before I went to bed, I read through a stack of prayer cards on my bedside table. Several saints were represented in the pile, and Mary was preeminent. Standing up against the base of the lamp was a picture of Jesus I had been awarded for winning a spelling bee. I certainly acknowledged the supremacy of Jesus, but hardly prayed directly to Him, being so convinced of my complete unworthiness to address Him. Mary and the saints, being fellow humans already successful in their quest for sainthood (we were taught) were the perfect mediators between us and a holy God. So I prayed diligently and sincerely to them, trusting they would use their influence with the Lord on my behalf, a sort of spiritual politics. I didn't know then, as a contemporary song puts it, that He was there all the time waiting for me to talk to Him. But He let me know just that one particular evening when I was preparing for bed.

I was getting ready to begin my series of prayers when my eyes were drawn to the picture of Jesus by the lamp. Sitting there looking at it, something I could not explain came over me and my attention was riveted on that card. In an instant of time, my "prayer life" was totally changed. I abandoned many of my prayers to the saints as a penetrating conviction unlike anything I had previously experienced took hold of me and made clear to me that I must pray to Jesus and not to all of those other people. He became approachable to me, my Friend, almost like a big brother. Years later I would discover that the Bible speaks of Him in these very terms, but at that time, it was a sovereign work of the Holy Spirit in my life, for I knew precious little of what the Bible had to say.

This conviction remained with me through the years, and though there were times when I still prayed the rosary, as we were obliged to do by the rule in the convent, my perspective on prayer and relating to Jesus was irreversibly altered. He became the center of my spiritual life, such as it was at that time. It wasn't complete deliverance, but a very important step in the direction which would later bring me into total truth.

Sixth grade was the year in which I first began to think seriously of becoming a nun. The thought was not new. My mother had already been encouraging it and the sisters in school were active in promoting their way of life. I dearly loved my sixth grade teacher, and she had a profound impact on my considerations. I began daily attendance at Mass at this time and did so for the remaining years of my schooling, even Saturdays. By sixth grade I had read enough lives of the saints to be sufficiently inspired to begin my own quest for sanctity, which I had already concluded was the most worthwhile goal in life. I prayed a great deal for an eleven year old, reading pages and pages of prayers to Jesus in whatever devotional books I could find then, and I dreamt about being a Sister of Mercy like the teachers I had.

I put up with seventh grade because I had to get through it to enter eighth. Math was terrible, and I didn't much care for the teacher. Of course, nobody was as good as last year's sister. Even if she was, I wouldn't have noticed. I knew there could never be as terrific a teacher as she, or so I thought until high school.

Eighth grade was traumatic. My teacher was an old school, knuckles-rapping nun who yelled a lot, threatened continually, and generally made school a trial. She had favorites, too; that was obvious, since I wasn't one of them!

Two things happened during this year that proved to be critical in determining future events in my life. A coed high school which accepted students from all the local Catholic schools was staffed by the Sisters of Mercy. I'd had my heart set on continuing my education there with these sisters. A change of administration coupled with a record number of applications that year resulted in a totally revamped admissions procedure, and though my marks were good, to my horror I was not accepted. Adding vinegar to the wound was the fact that Susan, one of the eighth grade "favorites," was accepted, and I knew her marks weren't as good as mine. It was a bitter pill to swallow, and I cried for days.

I was terrified of public school, somehow imagining it to be a fearful world populated with those "other people" who were on their way to hell. Wanting desperately to stay in my secure Catholic environment, the only option now was a small, private all girls' academy just over the river. It was expensive, very strict, and very French. It was also accepting new students.

The customs of the nuns at this school differed greatly from those of the Sisters of Mercy. These Sisters of the Sacred Hearts were a Paris-based order who wore white habits and funny white bonnets instead of black dresses and veils, spoke French as much as possible and were very old-worldish. It was a big change for me, but I was enrolled at great financial sacrifice to my parents.

The other significant event which took place when I was in the eighth grade was the arrival in town of five Sisters of the Holy Names from Albany, New York, to staff a new elementary school located just minutes from where I lived. This new school was opened by the parish of which my grandmother and aunts were members. The five newcomers had much to do, settling into a new convent and opening a new school. While totally devoted to my school and the Sisters of Mercy, I considered the Sisters of the Holy Names new friends and went by frequently to help them. My high school years and a new Superior at the Holy Names convent two years later would change the course of my life.

As I look back I see the hand of God at work even then. Had I gone to the high school of my choice, I would no doubt have entered the novitiate of the Sisters of Mercy in

Rhode Island. But God had a plan for me in Albany that He was about the business of accomplishing, though none of us involved could have foreseen a bit of the course of the next few years.

How marvelous are His ways, how inscrutable His designs.

IV

The Almost Reunion

"I don't believe you, Norma. I just don't believe you." Doria took another sip of the too hot coffee, put the cup down, and for the first time that morning relaxed as she rested her head against the back of the booth. The coffee shop was fairly empty, and only the sound of muffled conversation from several booths away broke the peaceful quiet. A lone waitress disappeared behind the swinging chrome door with its single smudged window. Doria took a long look at her dear friend, Norma, nervously puffing on the ever-present cigarette. Then she began to laugh quietly. Norma looked up, surprised, her concentration interrupted.

"What are you laughing about?" she queried. "I'm the

one who just bought the place. I must be crazy!" Norma said as she crushed another butt into the collection already spilling over the edge of the ash tray.

"No, Norma, you're not crazy," her friend responded. "You're just...Well, you're just...Norma!" she finished. Doria knew her well. They had been friends since childhood, and it was always Norma who did what others wished they could but didn't have the nerve. Who but the intrepid Norma would drive over to New Bedford, look at a property with a home and a restaurant, sign the papers to buy it with no money in her pocket (Doria had to buy the coffee!) and *then* wonder what Daddy would think! The uncanny part about it was that Norma always succeeded, and she would again. Of that, Doria was sure. How long it would last was another question, but that Norma would succeed, Doria had no doubts.

Early the next morning, Mr. Cleaves drove the twelve miles from home to the neighboring city and took a long, hard look at his favorite daughter's latest venture. Norma watched his face as he surveyed the property; a lovely two-family dwelling with spacious rooms, certainly enough to accommodate Norma and Judy as well as Daddy and Mother. Adjacent to the house stood a moderately sized diner, well-equipped but in need of sprucing up. A little paint and a lot of elbow grease would do wonders.

Daddy, with a low, deep sigh, turned to his adventurous Norma and, with a serious expression but a twinkle in his eye that betrayed his real feelings, told her all that she needed to know. "We'll have to hurry," he said simply. "The bank closes at noon today."

Three weeks later they were moving. Mother took care of settling in the house and interviewing prospective tenants for the first floor apartment while Norma busied herself with cleaning and refurbishing the diner. Daddy joined her when he came home at six after working all day at his vacuum cleaner establishment back in Fall River. Judy was conveniently enrolled in the Catholic school right across the busy thoroughfare from the diner. In short order Gus' Diner was ready for business.

Opening day was an exciting one for Norma. The local newspaper carried a sizable and inviting ad announcing the grand re-opening of Gus' Diner under new management. My mother noticed it as she looked over my shoulder at the newspaper I was reading that Friday night. "Maybe we can stop in there when we go shopping tomorrow," she volunteered. She knew how much I enjoyed eating out, even if it was at a simple hot dog stand, so I was pleased with her suggestion and looked forward to the morrow.

Saturday dawned bright and sunny. Up and down Acushnet Avenue shoppers bustled about with their purchases bulging precariously out of overstuffed shopping bags. We walked and shopped until we were tired. Just when I was convinced I couldn't walk another block, Gus' Diner came into view. We happily turned in to rest while we enjoyed a light lunch.

A pleasant looking blonde woman greeted us from behind the counter, and a pretty young girl washed dishes at the far end of the diner. I could tell she was a little older than I, and I can still remember her lovely brown hair.

"Judy," the waitress called from the back room, "Nana needs you upstairs." Judy held the swinging door open as our waitress came through, balancing coffee cups and plates on a metal tray. As she made her way to our table serving us cheerfully, Judy disappeared. We busied ourselves with the very welcome food.

I noticed that my mother seemed to be in a big hurry all of a sudden, and as I wiped mustard from my lips while struggling with the choice of pie or ice cream for dessert, my mother called for the check and said we really needed to be on our way. Lamenting over my lost dessert, I didn't notice how nervously my mother kept trying to conceal the ash tray on the table. She had spied it when the food was served and panic had gripped her. There on the rim were the words "Norma Cleaves, Proprietor."

As we had eaten, my mother had searched the waitress' face as boldly as she dared, looking for signs of resemblance, wondering if the blond hair was real or tinted, and refusing to admit how much of me she saw in the now absent Judy.

Our waitress smiled courteously as we left and commented on my big, brown eyes. It was the first time my real mother and I stood face-to-face since the day of my birth, though neither of us knew it. And it was the only time I saw my sister, Judy.

Meanwhile, in the quiet halls of my high school, somber-faced nuns demanded dignity, perfect manners, and European refinement from their students. We spoke French with a Parisian flair, conversed in Virgilian Latin, labored over geometric equations, and prayed in the chapel donned in our snow white veils that fell gracefully down our backs in marked contrast to crisp and spotless navy blue uniforms.

For some time during my high school years I considered entering this order of nuns, the Sisters of the Sacred Hearts, after graduation, but as my relationship developed with the sisters from Albany, I found myself increasingly drawn in the direction of the Sisters of the Holy Names instead.

In the summer of 1961, a new Superior was assigned to the New Bedford convent of the Holy Names, a very winsome lady who loved life and loved people. She quickly endeared herself to everyone, including me. Sister Elizabeth was young and vivacious, kind and understanding, compassionate and gentle, a friend in the true sense of the word to all whose lives she touched. Perhaps her most striking quality was that she was so real. She was the kind of person who caused you to like yourself better when you were with her.

We had some long talks on Saturdays when I would help her with routine school chores: correcting papers, decorating a bulletin board, and other such time-consuming tasks inherent in a teacher's responsibilities. As the Christmas of 1961 approached, Sister Elizabeth invited me to accompany her and the other sisters to New York for a few days during Christmas vacation. I could visit the motherhouse, see where the postulants and novices lived, meet the Mother Mistress and some of the other sisters. In short, I could take a close look at what the Sisters of the Holy Names had to offer. I was overjoyed, my parents consented, and I eagerly anticipated the trip.

Those few days in Albany were the turning point in my journey toward decision. I loved everyone and everything I saw. On my return home, I began counting off the weeks until I could call the novitiate home. My decision was sealed; I would serve God as a nun, and I would do it in Albany.

How long had I wanted to be a nun? As long as I can remember, I guess. Oh, I gave some thought as all girls do to marriage and children, but there was a very strong desire on my part to serve God. And in the framework of Roman Catholicism, the ideal way for a young woman to do this was to enter the convent. This was promoted as the "high calling," the way of sanctification and sainthood. My mother strongly supported this way of life and encouraged me so in this direction that I came to the point of believing that I would deeply disappoint her if I failed to enter the convent.

I would be hard pressed at this point to say which influence was the strongest in my decision to become a nun, but I do believe with all my heart that the Lord, whom I would come to know and serve, was even at this time directing and controlling every step of my journey to find Him, and it was He who directed me to Albany for His express purposes as they were later revealed.

The months passed quickly, examinations were taken, awards were presented, banquets and proms were held, and all manner of activities crowded the days during those last weeks until June 10, 1962, when our class of thirty-three seniors, robed in white academic gowns, nostalgically singing our alma mater for the last time, bid farewell to high school fun and friends. Some were married soon thereafter; many pursued higher education in institutions far and near; and four of us entered the religious life. Two stayed right in the Sacred Hearts convent, one went to another order in Taunton, and on July 2, I left for Albany, New York.

Sister Elizabeth obtained permission to make a special trip to drive me to the motherhouse and during the four-hour journey did her best to put me at ease and encourage me in the life I was about to enter. Her animated conversation seemed to shorten the miles, and the long day came to an end in that quiet and still dormitory of the Holy Names novitiate.

V

GIVE ME A BREAK!

"Tell me about yourself," she said, smiling that warm smile of hers that made every postulant melt into the chair. Mother Mistress had poured herself into the new recruits with all of her characteristic love and kindness, and now as my turn came for some time alone with her in her office, time to get better acquainted, I found myself singularly bereft of words. We talked a little about my parents, my high school, my decision to come to this place, and my friendship with Sister Elizabeth. She questioned me at length about my likes and dislikes, about what I saw as my strengths and weaknesses. I remember telling her of my love for languages, my love for writing, my dream of becoming an author and a poet, or maybe a French teacher.

All of this seemed to interest her very much at the time, though I could not understand why. I knew that once I entered the convent, my life was no longer my own. What I would study, when I would study, what I would wear, when I would sleep, when I would eat, what I would clean in the building—all of these would be decisions handed down arbitrarily from the Superior, that authority whom I was to train myself to hear, not as a human voice but as the voice of God Himself. The very bell which piercingly called us to our round of daily chores was to be to us the "call of God" to chapel, to laundry or to study. And well we were tested on our progress in learning this lesson.

I remember the day I had cleaned and polished the visitor's dining room until it shone like glass. The floors gleamed, the silver sparkled, the china glistened. An assistant Superior came by on an inspection tour. She looked over the room with meticulous care, then faced me squarely. With absolute seriousness in her icy blue eyes, she said, "Clean it again, Sister." With a swish of her robes, she was gone. That time I passed the test. Not even an eyelid flickered when she commanded me to repeat three hours of work I had just completed. Repeat it I did. Every piece of silver was polished again, just as if it had never been done. The floors had to have been the cleanest in all of New York State, washed and waxed a second time, and all under the watchful eye of a Superior who knew full well that it needed no second cleaning.

Weeks later she referred to that incident and told me I had succeeded in subduing my emotions to an "admirable level," and that if I continued the good work, I would most certainly be found worthy to be accepted into the next phase of training.

It is amazing to me today the things we were trained to

do in the name of holiness and Christlikeness, yet like a thirsty sponge I absorbed it all, never questioning, never resisting, being utterly convinced that following this way would make me the person I longed to be and would usher me into the relationship with Jesus I longed for and kept waiting for that relationship that seemed so long in coming.

Time passed quickly in the convent. There was always something to do. As college classes were pursued in earnest, the homework and paper writing common to all college students were added to our already heavy load of religious studies and duties. Ours was a teaching order so we were all being prepared to be educators. I endured one last battle with mathematics — college algebra. Oh, the rejoicing when that course ended! One would have thought that I had just been delivered from the lion's den; I'm sure I thought I was.

By this time a year had passed, and I was no longer the fresh-out-of-high-school postulant. I was Sister Mary Theresa of Jesus, a first year novice, dressed in the official garb of the order, minus the crucifix which was worn about the neck after pronouncing of vows and wearing a white veil in place of the black one I would receive at the end of my training.

If life was demanding as a postulant, it was more so as a novice. Increased community in this phase of training brought with it increased responsibility and restrictions. Life as a novice was austere, and the program for sanctification was intense. There was more penance, more discipline, more supervision, more studies, more of everything except free time! That became an unknown quantity.

My favorite time of day was early morning. Five thirty in the morning had become a friend to me over the previous year as I began to appreciate the time alone in the silence of the chapel. There I was alone with God; although surrounded by 300 other nuns, I was also alone with God. We were given specific meditation books, which I found difficult to use. More often than not my thoughts just turned to the Lord Himself and wondering why I didn't sense Him closer to me. Always resolving that it must be my fault, my daily resolution was to "try harder" to get closer to Jesus.

Yet even in my frustration those morning meditation times were very special and precious to me. It was the only time of day I really felt was mine to pray and think about this Lord I wanted to serve. So often I was at a loss for words, and now I look back on those times wishing I had possessed then the invaluable gift of praying in the Spirit. What spiritual warfare could have been waged in all those hours of quiet solitude. But God knew, and for His perfect reasons, I was not allowed the satisfaction of knowing His presence, of sensing His closeness, except on rare occasions.

Sometime during the novitiate the fact that I was musically inclined came to the attention of the Superior, and in addition to my college and religious duties, I was instructed to begin weekly organ lessons with the accompanying daily practice times. This proved to be another real blessing because the only organ was in the chapel, and my hour of practice easily became an hour of communing with God through music.

I loved the organ and took some time during those practice sessions to compose a few organ pieces. This delighted my organ teacher, an older sister extremely proficient in keyboard instruments, but who to her dismay lacked the ability to create new music. She strongly encouraged my efforts, and in May of that year, she asked me to play my latest composition, an organ recessional, at the end of the Mass on a special feast day. I was thrilled, but evidently my happiness was too obvious, my enjoyment of the organ too apparent. It was the last time I was allowed to touch the organ.

Against the protests of my teacher, lessons were terminated, and I was forbidden to continue musical instruction "lest you get puffed up and proud of your talent, Sister Theresa." Silently I accepted the direction, bowed to the Superior, and left the room. Painfully I determined to accept it as His will, embracing the hurt as best I could, fearful of offending God by not hearing His voice in the Superior's as we were trained to do.

The weeks grew into years, and before it seemed possible the eve of my profession of vows was upon me. The last ten days before the momentous occasion were spent on retreat, in silent solitude with God, neither speaking nor being spoken to except by the retreat leader who preached to us three times a day. The weight of the commitments we were about to make was striking. These vows of poverty, chastity and obedience would bind us to God in an almost irrevocable way and must be taken with full consent and understanding. These vows would constitute our "marriage" to Christ, each of us seeing ourselves as a bride of His. We were expected to anticipate this day as any young woman might rejoice at the coming of her wedding.

For ten long, quiet days we pondered again the responsibilities soon to be undertaken, though we'd been carefully schooled in their meaning for two years now. Poverty required that never again would I consider anything my own. The clothing I wore, the bed I slept in, the very toothbrush I used was not "mine"; I was to own nothing at any time. I could expect to receive whatever I needed from the common storehouse if and when the Superior gave permission. Any gift of goods or money was to be immediately surrendered to the office. Not even the undergarments we wore could have our names on them as they went into the common laundry pile. What was returned to us from the laundry was what we wore, regardless of size or condition. My life would be one of asking permission for just about every move I made and everything I needed.

Chastity required the least elaboration. Marriage was forever ruled out, and special relationships were taboo. That old spiritual bugaboo in religious life, a thing they called "particular friendships," was forbidden under this vow. In practice this meant that we were forbidden to treat any one sister differently from any other. Despite natural preference for one personality over another, the truly holy sister was never to show partiality. We were to have no close friends, no confidants; God alone was our Friend. If we found ourselves feeling more affection for one sister we were to severely discipline that tendency in ourselves. Otherwise it would be disciplined by the Superiors, usually by having one of the sisters involved in a close friendship transferred to some distant city.

Obedience was the vow posing the biggest challenge on a day-to-day basis. Training oneself to accept *every* event of *every* day, 365 days a year, as the direct call of God; to overlook personalities, especially in the Superiors, and to see God in them — now *that* was a monumental task!

When commands were given that were obviously illogical or even ridiculous, obedience demanded that ever present stoic look and a prompt, "Yes, Mother." When the bell rang for chapel, study or dinner, obedience dictated that one should jump to one's feet and move as if it were a fire bell. When the annual appointments were read and Sister So-and-So who was a trained musician was appointed to teach junior high school science for which she was totally unprepared, obedience demanded that she be promptly on her way to this new assignment with nary a word of resistance or complaint.

Yes, this vow of obedience was something to consider, yet as the eve of my profession was upon me and I weighed the requirements well, I was eager for the next morning, having arrived at the decision that if this was what it took to draw close to God and to serve Him well, then it would be eminently worth the effort and sacrifice that was required.

Once I pronounced my vows and sealed my intentions publicly, perhaps then I would begin to know that closer intimacy with God that I'd been seeking. Perhaps then I would know what it was to feel His presence. I went to bed that night very excited about the morrow. My long awaited dream was about to come true.

The ceremony the next day, climaxing two years of intense study and discipline, was attended by our family and friends. Each of us in the class felt a certain satisfaction in reaching this milestone in our journey toward final vows which we expected to pronounce five years later.

We would spend two more years at the motherhouse completing our college degree in education and simultaneously increasing our knowledge and practice of the traditional disciplines of monastic life before being assigned to teach in one of the many schools staffed by our order along the eastern seaboard of the United States.

VI

Treasure in a Paperback

"Sister Theresa, we only have room for six in the car, so as the youngest in the house, you will have to stay home." The words stung, but I bowed in submission. "Yes, Sister Superior," I responded.

"There's a good bit of laundry downstairs which you could get done while we are gone, and I'm sure you have homework, so use your time wisely. I expect to see much accomplished by tonight," she concluded.

With that, Sister Superior and the other five nuns swept through the door and out to the car on their way to the local cinema for a special showing of *The Sound of Music.* It was April 1967, and a movie showing arranged just for the benefit of the nuns in the area was very unusual. When word of the invitation had come several days earlier, we were exuberant. For most of us, it had been several years since we had seen a movie of any kind, and the fact that the Provincial Superior had given permission for our community to accept the invitation was indeed an event unprecedented in the annals of the sisterhood.

We'd talked of nothing else in the few days leading up to that special Saturday. Through the morning all of us had raced about completing our chores for the day, cleaned up the kitchen after the noon meal in record time, and readied ourselves for the grand and unusual outing.

At the last minute as the seven of us stood ready to leave, I was suddenly left out. I watched as the blue station wagon pulled out of the driveway and turned in the direction of the theater, not too far from our particular convent. Now that I was alone, my tears could fall and none would be the wiser. Anger welled up inside of me while hot tears burned down my cheeks. I flew down to the laundry and filled three washing machines with a vengeance.

"A good bit of laundry," I muttered. "My foot, this is nothing. She knows right well I do twelve loads every Wednesday. Why did she have to do it like that? Why couldn't she have told me earlier that I wasn't going?"

Wearily I climbed the stairs to the first floor, then the second. I went into my little room, closed the door, fell down on my knees beside the bed and had a good, long cry.

"Oh, God, why am I still like this? Why do I still get angry? When am I ever going to learn? Oh, God, I'm sorry...I'm sorry." As my emotions subsided and found release in tears, I again became discouraged at my total inability to be what I thought a holy nun should be. Oh, I knew that some of the other nuns jokingly called me "Sister Perfection." I had mastered the externals pretty well, but I wasn't satisfied. Something inside me was not content that I observed all the rules and hardly flinched anymore at the humiliations of the Chapter of Faults.

I knew, and somehow I knew God knew, that inside it was different. I still hurt, I still got angry, I still felt resentful at too many of those things; somehow it didn't ring true to me that the externals were enough. Too often we were told that it was not the feelings we had on the inside that mattered. Feelings were human; perfection consisted in very systematically gaining control over those feelings; as we grew in control, gradually even the feelings would no longer be there. So we poured our energies into this Spartan-type discipline.

"Sisters: The perfect religious never allows another person to know her true feelings. The perfect religious never shows any but the proper responses at the proper times. The perfect religious is in total control of feelings and emotions at all times. And to reach this state of perfection you can expect to be tested over and over again."

We'd heard it so much we could say it in our sleep; I'd been tested again this very day, and in the Superior's eyes I'd probably passed the test by my stoic response to a crushing disappointment. Yet something about it didn't ring true. I still felt unfulfilled, dissatisfied, and empty, and in some way, untrue and dishonest before God. Meticulously disciplined on the outside for all the nuns to see, yet battling these negative forces on the inside.

Deep down I knew God wasn't fooled, and it tormented me to think that when the Day of Judgment came, He just might not have the same criteria of evaluation that Sister Superior had. There was an increasing, unsettling fear in my heart that God might not be satisfied with external observance and "control," but that He might be more concerned with a heart that was *really* humble, free of bitterness and anger, and able to receive disappointments with a sweetness of spirit.

I pushed the thoughts from my mind. I didn't like the way it made me feel to think like that. After all, wasn't I in the most spiritually secure place in the world? If I couldn't be holy here, it must be totally impossible elsewhere.

I went over to my window and looked out. The sky was a deep blue with not a cloud in sight. My gaze took in the panorama of the complex before me: a church, a school, a rectory housing three priests, a huge parking lot that was always filled on Sundays, and our small enclosed backyard behind the convent I now called home.

I seemed hard to believe that almost two years had passed since I'd come here, armed with a teaching degree and religious vows, full of enthusiasm for my new opportunity to serve Christ in the classroom.

At the end of my training, my first assignment beyond the walls of the motherhouse had brought me to this local parish, to a small convent of seven nuns, including the Superior. It was quite a change from the motherhouse with its large population of more than three hundred.

There was Sister Superior, a very withdrawn woman in her fifties who rarely smiled and who frowned on too much happiness in anybody else. Sister Julia, on the other hand, was a dear woman who'd already labored in the classroom some forty years. She was especially helpful to the young sisters just beginning their teaching careers, giving of her time generously to help them overcome problems. Everyone loved Sister Julia.

Then there were the five of us, all relatively close in age. I was grateful not to have been put in a convent where all the nuns were significantly older. I thought of Sister Rose, one of my classmates in the novitiate, who had been sent to Florida and was living with six other nuns — she in her twenties and the other five all over sixty! Poor Sister Rose. Lord, help her!

I enjoyed teaching fifth grade, and now in the second year in the same classroom, I found it considerably easier. The children were responsive, interested for the most part, and classroom discipline was not a major problem. I poured myself into my teaching, driven in this too by my desire to work my way to heaven and holiness.

Yet while everything seemed to be going well for me both in the convent and in the classroom, I could not escape the nagging doubts inside me. Why, why, why did I have this empty ache? Where was the peace and serenity?

I examined myself over and over. Where was I failing? What was I not doing that I should be doing? Repeatedly I pondered the torturous question. I reasoned that the answer must somehow lie in the area of prayer. Arriving at the conclusion from all my reading that the great saints spent long hours praying, I had begun some weeks earlier to rise an hour before the rest of the community to spend the extra time in the chapel. Each morning I would silently wend my way downstairs and into the front pew where only a red vigil light flickered at the front of the tiny sanctuary. There I would kneel and fight sleepiness to pray and seek God. It seemed as though the words fell from my lips with a thud on the floor in front of me as day after day I followed my self-imposed schedule of extended prayer, coupled with increased penitential practices in a desperate attempt to get some kind of answer from God concerning my discontent.

Thank God for His incomparable wisdom and patience. His grace wouldn't allow me to meet Him then, for I would have forever remained bound in the chains of "works." Thank God that He's God and that His thoughts are higher than ours.

I turned from my window to the pile of books on my

desk. I was enrolled in a Monday evening class at the local college, beginning to accumulate some post-graduate credits. The teacher assigned enough homework for three courses. I flipped through the pages of a resource book I had borrowed from the library and began to read. At the end of the page I realized that I couldn't remember a word I'd read, so I put the book down and slumped back in the chair. I rested in the silence of the house for a few minutes, eyes closed, mind blank. Perhaps some quiet time in the chapel would bring peace to my troubled soul, I thought, and I made my way downstairs.

Summer came and went that year and my restlessness wore on. I was going into my seventh year in the convent now, reassigned to the same local convent for another year, and conscious of the very important twelve months ahead of me, perhaps the most important since I'd entered the order. At the end of the seven years the irrevocable decision must be made. The time for consideration and doubt must come to an end, and the Final Vows of religious life spoken or the life forsaken.

This final decision was two-fold: for the sister, a decision for this lifestyle and in this community till death; and for the order, its affirmation to be responsible for said sister and to receive her into the ranks of its lifetime members. Her conduct over the past seven years had been carefully scrutinized and recorded. Her file would be thoroughly reviewed by the Provincial Council, a group of several nuns who, with the Provincial Superior, form the governing body of the community. Their unanimous approval of each candidate was mandatory before the Final Vows could be pronounced by the individual.

As the new school year got underway and I began to acquainted with my third set of fifth graders, it was with somewhat of a heavy heart that I surveyed the year to come.

Knowing full well that I was not at peace, but at a loss to know what to do, I turned to the counsel of a local priest, feeling sure he must have the answer I needed. I described to him my concerns, my disappointment at not finding fulfillment, peace, joy and a sense of God's love. He listened kindly and then shared the best of what he had after thirty-eight years in the priesthood. I will never forget what he said.

"Sister Theresa, you are trying too hard. Be content with observing your Holy Rule, knowing that God wants nothing more from you. I have not found fulfillment, peace or joy in all my years of the priesthood either. I think you expect too much. Life here below is, after all, a vale of tears. Just be faithful to what you know and expect no more here below. It will come later if hopefully we persevere to the end and God has mercy and receives us into His kingdom."

I left his presence totally dejected. If he were right, how terribly depressing life on this earth must really be.

Perhaps I *was* expecting too much; perhaps life was meant to be hard and dry and lonely; perhaps that was part of the "call"; perhaps such a life was supposed to make you holy in the end. Funny, I'd never read that in the lives of the saints, but perhaps, I reasoned, good writers purposely omitted it lest the ready be discouraged from embarking on such a spiritual journey.

I marvel at how carefully the Lord was ordering and directing each step and preparing me for what He was about to do in my life in the next few months and years. As I remember how dark and bleak I felt that day, I marvel even more at His keeping grace even before I knew Him.

In my class that year was a charming little girl with an equally charming mother. Suzanne had a Catholic father and so was enrolled in Catholic school and reared in the Catholic church, but her mother was a Baptist — and a very devoted evangelical one at that. We nuns loved her because she was most generous with her time in helping out at the school, doing favors for the sisters, baking special goodies for us from time to time, and being an all-around delightful person. We used to remark on her sweet disposition though she was one of those Protestants, and some of the sisters prayed fervently for her "conversion" to Catholicism.

I remember one particular day that Mrs. Nattelle came to the convent door with a delicious apple pie for our dinner that evening. Having received it and graciously thanked her, the sister brought it into the kitchen where two of us were preparing salad, saying, "Let's take a minute to pray for Mrs. Nattelle. What a shame that such a lovely person will go to hell if she doesn't become a Catholic. Hail, Mary, full of grace...." Such was the absolute belief in Roman doctrine that was pumped into us. I was already beginning to feel very uncomfortable with these concepts and prayed silently that God would bless our benefactor in any way He chose to do so.

In late October of that year on one of those lovely Indian summer afternoons that make children laugh with glee as they kick their way home through the piles of richly colored leaves, Mrs. Nattelle was busily correcting a mountain of math papers for me as I prepared the next day's lessons, racking my brain for creative ways to make fifth grade boys interested in present and past participles and ancient history. A quick look at the schoolroom clock jarred my concentration, and I hastily called over to my dutiful assistant, "Oh, my, I really must hasten. It's 4:30, and I have to have supper on the table at 5:15."

I haphazardly stuffed my books and papers into the oversized black satchel, and as we started to leave, making sure that all the windows were locked, Mrs. Nattelle paused, stretched one hand out to me and said, "Sister

Theresa, I notice you never carry your big Bible around, so I thought maybe you would like this. See you tomorrow." With that, she was gone.

There I stood with a pocket-sized American Bible Society copy of the *Good News for Modern Man*. With the pressure of getting supper ready on time, I quickly dropped it into my deep pocket, well hidden under several layers of flowing black skirts, and postponed the decision as to how I would handle the situation.

Later in the evening, with meal time and prayer time behind me, I retrieved the little paperback from my pocket and in the privacy of my room pondered the decision that needed to be made. Mrs. Nattelle's gift threw me into a dilemma. Our vow of poverty precluded the receiving of any personal gifts at any time. All that came to us was to be surrendered to the Superior.

The reason Mrs. Nattelle never saw us carrying our "big Bibles" around was because we didn't have one to carry. In our particular order we were discouraged from reading the Bible, being instructed that it was to be left in the hands of the theologians. We were reminded that reading the Bible had been at the root of Martin Luther's problem and had caused the deplorable schism in the church from which we still suffered today. That was the cause of hundreds of people suffering damnation who were "torn" from the true Church because one man decided to interpret the Bible for himself. (As the saying goes, Martin Luther must have rolled over in his grave!)

Consequently, the Bibles that did exist in the convent were kept in the library and each time we wanted to read a portion, we were required to seek permission, informing the Superior what passages we wanted to read and why. It generally needed to be associated with some assignment from a theology class or the permission would be denied, and we would be told to restrict our reading to the spiritual books assigned to us.

Now as I sat on the edge of the bed, holding the New Testament in my hands, I was conscious of a tremendous struggle within. Should I turn it in to the Superior? Or should I give in to the strong desire I was feeling to keep it and read it for myself?

Sometime in the course of my life, I had come to the conviction that the Bible was indeed the inspired Word of God. Holding a portion of it there in my hands, I was overwhelmed with the desire to devour it from cover to cover. I knew it was out of the question according to normal practice, but why should it be?

Puzzled and a bit confused by the Rule to which I was committed, I slid off the bed and sank to my knees. In my ignorance I prayed the only prayer that made any sense to me that night.

"God, I really do believe that this is Your Word; and if that's true, I don't understand why we should be forbidden to read it freely. I really want to know what's true, Lord, so I'm going to keep this Bible here in my room and read it every night. If it's really displeasing in Your sight, then let me get caught by the Superior and I'll take the consequences. But if I can get through the whole New Testament without anyone finding out I'm reading it on my own, then I'm going to take that as a solid statement from You that it's all right to read the Bible, and I'll know the Rule is wrong."

With the amen to that naïve prayer, I felt a peace that surprised me. I, the one who had been scrupulously obeying every jot and tittle of the Rule, was able this time to lay it aside and be at peace. I wondered about that momentarily, then hungrily delved into the little book in my hands. I didn't get too far that night, but when the bell rang for lights out and the commencement of Grand Silence, I quickly tucked away my hidden treasure in the bottom drawer and climbed into bed, happier than I'd been in a long time.

Days melted into weeks and weeks into months. Every available moment I could find, I would sneak away to my room and read the Bible. After a few weeks, as certain passages really struck me, I began to read with the Bible in one hand and the Rule book in the other, comparing and analyzing, asking questions that no human being could answer. The list of contradictions and inconsistencies between the two books was getting longer and longer, and it was becoming increasingly difficult to continue to view the Holy Rule in the way I had been instructed these past six and a half years. This accumulation of 258 rules which we memorized and applied ourselves to master as the ultimate means for becoming Christlike now seemed to have lost all authority. Their impact on my life paled in the light of the Gospel I now read.

Unregenerate though I was, the amazing grace of which the songwriter speaks was poured out into my life at that time, and the Bible came alive to me. Sovereignly the Holy Spirit illumined key concepts and passages which showed me beyond the shadow of a doubt that His Word and the Rule book were mutually exclusive.

There was a sense in which this was very frightening; but there was a greater sense in which it was amazingly liberating. While I would not come to know Jesus as Savior and Lord for some months yet, during that fall and winter while I diligently poured all my available time into His Word, I began to feel a peace and a sense of the beginning of the fulfillment I had been seeking.

And Sister Superior never caught me! Though we had regular room inspection and she could have walked in on me at any time when I was reading, she never did, and I wonder if an angel didn't blind her eyes to the small paperback Bible in my bottom drawer when she did her inspections.

By early February I had completed my reading of Revelation and had a notebook full of questions which I had already begun to answer through reading the Scriptures.

In mid-March we who were due for Final Vows that summer would be summoned for our preliminary examination before the Provincial Council. Well in advance of the day, I knew what I must do. It was at once an exciting yet terrifying thought. I had come to the decision that, at least for me, a living relationship with God was not to be found within these walls. I had come to believe that God had something else for me and that I needed to make myself available to seek that out with all my heart. That was the exciting part.

Coupled with it was the awesome realization that I didn't have the slightest idea where else to start looking for God. My whole life had been built around the doctrine that the Roman church was the only church, and outside of it there was no salvation. The last few years had been lived on the premise that the convent was the closest place to heaven and the greatest means of sanctification.

Yet as I had read the Gospels and the letters of Paul, it became crystal clear to me that salvation came from knowing Jesus Christ, not from membership in any given church. I began to notice that Jesus Himself had been very severe with the "professional" religious of His day, and He was especially intolerant of external practices which did not come from a heart of love.

These realities and many others akin to them had stirred me deeply, and I prepared to face the Council with a good bit of trepidation. Their questions would be shrewd, their arguments difficult to refute with words. I just knew that I knew that somewhere beyond these walls there was another life for me and that God would lead me to it. That much I believed with all my heart.

My first meeting with the members of the Council seemed interminable. To the traditional opening question, "Sister, the time has come for you to state your intentions. What is your decision?" I responded, "I have deliberated and prayed over this matter for several months and I have decided to leave this convent at the expiration of my temporary vows."

They stared in disbelief. They had expected the traditional answer to their traditional question. Shock gave way to an outburst of pleadings.

"Sister Theresa, surely you can't be serious?"

"What has gotten into you?"

"You will be turning your back on God's calling," another offered. "Think of your family and how proud your parents are to have a nun in the family."

"Surely the devil is deceiving you; you must turn your back on him in this time of temptation."

On and on it went. I sat silently, secretly hoping that they would not press me too much, being convinced that if I ever told them I was leaving the convent because I had read the Bible they just might take a notion to confining me in the convent infirmary for a period of "rest" and psychological testing!

Several meetings later, all their persuasive arguments exhausted, I was finally dismissed from their presence after one of the Superiors looked me squarely in the eyes and said, "We have done all we know do to do deter you from this course of action, but we have come to the conclusion that if you are so determined to follow through with this decision, we must commend you to God and give you our blessing. We will pray for you, and we hope that you will pray for us. May God go with you."

With that ordeal behind me, I plunged into the balance of the school year with a new sense of freedom and lightheartedness. By April I began making some contacts for a possible job in the fall, teaching in a public school or perhaps as a lay teacher in another parochial school. All of this had to be done in great secrecy for it was against the Holy Rule to inform any of the other sisters that we were planning to leave, even those with whom we lived so closely, "lest they also be tempted."

There was so much to consider. Seven years of cloistered living had not prepared me to assume my place in the "outside world." I had no idea what food and clothing costs were, where to shop, and how to converse with everyday people when I knew nothing of current events. Television and newspapers were not allowed. It was literally a matter of going from one world to another.

VII

FREE, TRULY FREE

The school year ended on June 10 of 1969, and I was to be released from my vows on June 21. A scant few weeks before that date, Pentecost Sunday dawned bright and beautiful. The Mass was an elaborate celebration that morning, and because it was one of the great feasts of the church year, we were allowed to speak during a special breakfast of bacon, eggs, and sweet rolls, a menu reserved for only the most noteworthy days during the year.

Spring was in the air, and spring was in my heart. I remember feeling a lightness and buoyancy with me on that morning, not realizing as I cleaned up the kitchen what a unique day it would prove to be in God's unfolding plan for my life.

It was always quiet in our convent on Sunday afternoons. Those few hours between the noon meal and our late afternoon common recreation hour constituted our weekly appointment with privacy, the only time we were really free to do as we pleased — nap, read, write letters, or try our hand at knitting or some other handiwork.

This particular Sunday I chose the chapel. It was empty and the best place I could find for some extended reflection. Among the practical aspects of my impending adventure into life were some sobering thoughts that had been vying for my attention.

Now that I knew what I didn't want to do with my life, what *did* I want? Loneliness was not appealing, and pictures of happily married young couples with bright-eyed children, such as those I saw in our parish church every week, floated across my mind.

Fear and desire make for a strange mixture of emotions. Desire I knew I had, but fear at the prospect of marriage was very real. I had been raised, you see, in a very protective environment. I had not dated as a teenager, and adding to my social and romantic inexperience were fears generated by reports of failed marriages and broken homes among some of my high school friends. I shuddered. What did I know that would equip me for such a weighty decision? How could tell if a man would be a faithful husband and a committed father? And what of me? Where would I learn what I needed to know in order to be the kind of wife a man would be proud of? The kind of mother children really needed?

I groaned inside. A sense of inadequacy flooded my conscious mind. I voiced my conflicts before the Lord, afraid of being alone for the rest of my life and yet more afraid of making a deplorable choice. I remember thinking that although I had chosen the convent seven years earlier and given it my all, it had proved to be less than what I had dreamed. Yet it had been a breakable commitment. It had not worked out, and now I was free to go.

But marriage wasn't like that, at least not for me. Marriage was the point of no return. Marriage was for keeps. In a disposable society, marriage was still a permanent institution. That, at least, was the only kind of marriage I was interested in having.

The rush of thoughts subsided and I sat quietly, drinking in the silence, sensing a peace that softly filled my soul. A decision was forming in my consciousness, and a prayer expressed my innermost thoughts.

"Lord," I whispered, "You know I don't really want to be alone for the rest of my life, but I don't know the first thing about finding the right husband, and I don't want to make a mistake. Lord, please; if I'm ever going to marry, I'm really going to need Your help. I need to depend on you, and somehow show me, please, so I don't make a mistake."

I pondered the words I'd just prayed in the soothing calmness of the chapel. A soft breeze coming in the window carried the lilting song of a happy little bird perched on a branch of our fragrant lilac bush. In the midst of this delightful serenity, a gentle male voice from the back chapel spoke these words aloud:

"The one who baptizes you will be the one I have chosen."

Startled, frightened, perplexed, confused—I was all of these at once. I jerked my head around quickly, but there was no one there. I noticed myself trembling as I took in the perimeters of the chapel with a sweeping glance. There was no one there.

I sank back into the pew and just sat.

For long time I just sat.

Slowly that inner peace I'd begun to know returned, and though I did not understand how, why or what had precisely happened, I was convinced that God had spoken to me. It made no sense to the theology I knew then, but I could not shake the reality of what had happened. After some time I committed the experience to God, deciding very logically that if indeed He had spoken to me, He was very capable of explaining what He said when I needed to know. I put it on the shelf, as it were, and as the hours of Sunday solitude were coming to a close, I made my way to the kitchen and the simmering pot of spaghetti sauce on the stove.

The end of the school year is always a hectic time for teachers, and this year was no exception. In addition to compiling reports, grading end of the year exams, cleaning the classrooms, and other such multiple duties, I was busily snatching minutes here and there to make myself two dresses. Of course, all my sewing had to be done in great secrecy and privacy, lest any of the sisters catch a glimpse of my pretty green and white print fabric. Certainly that would be a dead giveaway!

As I waved goodbye to my forty-eight fifth graders on that last day of school, I did so with the proverbial lump in my throat, knowing that I would probably never see any of them again. The Nattelle family had moved during the year and were now in a distant city, not available to be told after I left that I would not be back in the fall. I did take care to obtain their new address and looked forward to writing them later. I wanted Mrs. Nattelle to know what a tremendous impact that casually given New Testament had on my life.

I had studiously cleaned my classroom every day for the past week, so I had nothing left to do on that final day except to pack up the last of my few belongings and lock the door. My departure from the convent was scheduled for noon thc next day while the sisters were in chapel for prayers before lunch.

I spent most of Friday afternoon in my room, packing, unpacking, and repacking the few things I would be allowed to take with me out of the convent: one set of bath towels, an extra pair of nylon stockings, a few underthings, a pair of light pink pajamas, the black bedroom slippers and robe which were already quite worn, some college notebooks, and the pink dress I'd finished sewing the previous evening. I'd decided to wear the green and white print on the morrow.

The black suitcase was hardly full, but tucked in one corner was that precious New Testament. I really didn't care now if anybody saw it. I was proud of it. It had brought me peace and liberty, and I instinctively knew there was more peace and liberty ahead as I continued to study that little book.

By nightfall the tile floor of my room was waxed to a shine, the walls and windows sparkled, and the curtains had been washed, pressed and re-hung. I crawled into bed for the last time, tired, happy, excited, and nervous.

The morning hours flew. It took me some time to arrange my shoulder length hair which I had been secretly allowing to grow for several months. The green and white print fit pretty well, though I decided the hem was a little too long. No matter, I could adjust it later. It was difficult to assess how I looked in the small mirror, but for what I could see, I looked mighty strange to myself. I rejoiced that I looked much younger without the habit than with it. I wondered if others would think so as well.

The bell rang at precisely at 11:40 as it always did. They would not miss me in chapel since I always stayed in the kitchen at that time making final preparations for the noon meal which was served at 12:15.

Today, however, I slipped down the back stairs at 11:55, shook hands with the Superior who was waiting for me there, stole a furtive glance down the hallway in the direction of the chapel, then walked out into the sunshine and a waiting car.

I heard the unmistakable click of the lock behind me and momentarily panicked as the finality of the step through the convent threshold became very real. With a deep breath, I lifted my head, squared my shoulders and walked with determination to the open car door. It was a short ride to the home where I was to spend the weekend relaxing and adjusting to my new surroundings until I traveled on Monday to Massachusetts and my parents.

Sister Superior had handed me an envelope with $200 in it as I left that morning. After a pleasant lunch with my hostess, we took some time to get acquainted with each other during my first visit to a mall in seven years. I was like a child in a candy shop. Racks and racks of pretty, colorful clothes almost made me dizzy after the austere black and white. I found it difficult to make a choice. Three hours and two cups of coffee later, we returned home with only a pair of sandals, a casual skirt of soft yellow and a top to match.

Then I spent two weeks with my parents. My dad was delighted to have me home, though concerned about my future plans.

My mother, however, was having great difficulty adjusting to my withdrawal from religious life. Generally speaking, most Catholic parents find great comfort and pride in their offspring who follow the way of the priesthood or the convent. It is a vehicle of religious security, God's ultimate mark of approval on their parenting. Consequently when a son or daughter leaves the priesthood or nunnery, it is an emotionally charged crisis in the life of the parents as well.

It was all of that for my mother. There was a certain amount of embarrassment, humiliation, and that dreaded thing called failure. That was, after all, pretty much the way it was regarded. We who left the convent were looked upon as having failed to "make the grade." It was a very tense situation, not at all helped by my own insecurity and uncertainty as I tried to adjust.

Having obtained a teaching position in Troy, New York, I decided in mid-July to return to Albany, stay with the family who had hosted me when I first left the convent, and find some peace of mind and a place to live. The Lord was so faithful to me when I did not yet know Him. Within a day of returning to Albany, I met another young woman teacher who was looking for a roommate to share an apartment. We easily located a charming place with two bedrooms, a bright and airy living room, efficient kitchen, and a very pink bathroom, perfectly suited to two young women. We liked it immediately, and Annette very kindly paid the deposit since my funds were so limited. I was having to make that $200 stretch until September 15, when I would receive my first paycheck. I would make it up to her later.

Meanwhile I kept in touch with my parents by phone and letter. My mother was still very disturbed about my leaving the convent, my taking a job so far from home, and my sharing an apartment with someone she did not know — all of which flew in the face of their Portuguese traditions and customs.

On my part, I felt a deep need to be on my own, to do some searching for myself, to break away from the Catholic mold and framework, all of which would be exceedingly difficult back in New Bedford.

I tried to express my feelings and desires, but emotional

involvements have a way of blurring rational and productive communication. My parents and I went through a painful time of hurt and misunderstanding on both sides. They were finding it hard to let go of their little girl who had changed tremendously in those seven years away and was now a woman trying to resolve some very basic issues of life. I expected too much from them and was hurt and resentful that they couldn't understand and accept me where I was.

Time and time alone is the great arbiter of conflict, and as time passed we learned to communicate again, to understand each other once more. They learned to let go of me and let me grow. I learned that little girls will always be little girls in their parents' eyes, and that's all right.

I was also beginning to learn during this time that the Gospel of Jesus Christ makes demands that supersede even devotion to family, and that in choosing His direction for my life, I had to be willing to stand in the face of criticism and misunderstanding from those I most expected to support me.

With the pressure of dealing with my parents, adjusting to life, facing responsibilities hitherto unknown to me, and still without a saving knowledge of Jesus Christ and His indwelling presence, those first weeks home found me under considerable strain.

By July 17 I was extremely depressed and discouraged. All the joyous promise of a new life had fled — I wasn't sure where — and gloom was the order of the day. I felt very alone, very abandoned, and very lost. I tried to read the New Testament that had been so alive to me before, and now it seemed only words on a page.

Annette noticed that morning how downcast I was, and over a cup of coffee she gingerly suggested that perhaps I might like someone to talk to, someone who could pray with me.

Now that was a novel idea. It caught my interest—someone who could pray *with* me. All my life people had said they would pray *for* me; no one had ever spoken of praying *with* me.

I listened as she continued. She explained that she was involved in a prayer meeting and knew some fine Christian people, one or two in particular who she thought could help. Almost apologetically she mentioned that they were Protestants and hoped that wouldn't matter to me. She pressed on eagerly to tell me that they were wonderful people and I really should get to know them. Could she call and see if someone was available for a visit?

It was the first bright spot in some days so I agreed, thinking it would be refreshing to hear what Protestants said about God since I'd never had opportunity to find out before. I'd never spoken to a Protestant about God before. Hard to believe, but true.

She excused herself from the room and returned just a few minutes later with a curious smile playing about her lips. Yes, she'd made contact, and one of the two leaders she'd had in mind was home and available. We were both invited over for a simple supper after which he and I could talk.

After the quick drive to Schenectady, a smiling, very old and very little lady answered the door and welcomed us into her home. It was obvious that Annette was acquainted with Mrs. Slocum, who explained that her grandson would be out in a moment and would we please make ourselves at home in the front room while she put the finishing touches on our dinner.

Moments later Annette introduced me to a young man named Mike, who greeted me with a warm smile and whose very distinctive hazel eyes seemed to look right through me.

I felt comfortable in his presence, and we exchanged small talk as we joined his grandmother at the kitchen table. I perceived quickly from the conversation that he and Annette had many friends in common, and I surmised that this prayer meeting of which she spoke must be a very important part of their lives, so enthusiastically did they converse about their associations there. The discussion was liberally peppered with "Praise the Lord" and "Hallelujah," and I felt somewhat out of place, almost as if I needed to learn a new language in order to talk to them.

Annette left quickly after we ate, and Mike suggested we take a ride since there were several people in the house and no place was good for quiet conversation.

As we drove, he drew me out with some simple questions about the convent, my home, my parents, and my background. Little by little I relaxed and found myself opening up to this total stranger — I, who was normally very shy and timid. I became more and more comfortable as I shared my frustration with convent life, my emptiness on the inside, my restlessness, my inability to please God or feel acceptable in His sight, my misgivings about Catholicism and its theology, my great sense of guilt and unworthiness.

On and on I talked as though someone had wound me up for extended play. He listened attentively, politely, seeming to really understand. Finally I stumbled over my words to an awkward halt and looked helplessly over at him, slightly embarrassed and not knowing what to say or do next.

Very quietly he began to speak. It was his turn now, and he spoke with an assurance and a confidence that I could sense was unshakable. His gentle manner underscored by contrast the impact of the words he spoke.

"You are a sinner, Barbara. You are unworthy, you are

guilty, you are empty, you are responsible for the death of Jesus. But the Good News is that by His death He set you free. His blood which you caused to be shed, which I caused to be shed, washes away your unworthiness, cleanses away your guilt, fills your emptiness with Himself, and makes you brand new. The Bible calls it being a new creature in Christ.

"You've been looking and looking and looking and now you're frustrated, but it's not His fault. You can find Him tonight, right now. It's not in theology, it's not in the working your way to heaven or to acceptability that you'll find Him. It's coming to grips with the eternal truth of the Word of God that it's not by our works that we are saved, but it's by His grace and goodness, by His blood that paid the price for you.

"You see, Romans chapter 8 says that there is *no* condemnation for those who are in Christ Jesus. You've been walking around for years under a load of condemnation that's been crushing you because you aren't equipped to carry it. Jesus already did.

"When you find Him, you are released from condemnation by confessing what you've proven to yourself, that you are unable to do it by yourself, that you need Him. You find Him by repenting and turning from doing your own thing your own way and accepting Him and His ways; you find Him by saying, 'Jesus, forgive me of all my sins, receive me into Your kingdom. I give You my life. Come into my heart and fill me with Yourself; make me what You want me to be and make my life count for You."

I leaned forward on the inside. Something in me was saying, *Yes, yes, yes — that's it, that's it!* I thought of the hundreds of sermons I had listened to in the convent, yet not one of these priests spoke about Jesus as this man spoke. Why, it was as if Jesus were his best Friend, the Man next door, a close acquaintance. He really *knew* Him.

He shared several scriptures with me, verses I had read but had not fully understood. I saw it. I could be free. I really could.

"Do you want this relationship with Him?"

"Yes, yes, that's what I've been looking for, but I don't know how."

"It's very simple, Barbara, yet it will cost you the rest of your life. You need to be willing to tell the Lord that it's all the way with Him, that you want Him to be your Savior, but also your Lord. That means He's the boss. You obey His Word because He's the boss. You turn away from what displeases Him because He's the Lord, because He paid for you with His own life's blood. It's a serious commitment and should not be made lightly. If that's what you want, if you really want Him, we can pray right now."

I knew the alternatives too well. There really was no choice to make. Eternal life and relationship with Jesus or more of the pain, frustration and emptiness I'd known for years. Now was not too soon. I wanted Him and I wanted Him now.

We pulled off the road into a beautiful park. It was early evening, and the sun was a warm, glowing red. I bowed my head, and Mike led me in prayer. Off to the left was a beautiful life-sized statue of the risen Christ coming out of the tomb. To my amazement I learned that this was not a park at all, but a burial estate, a cemetery! What a marvelous place to leave the old man and become a new creature in Christ Jesus, which is exactly what happened to me!

Everyone who has come to a saving knowledge of the Lord has a unique experience to relate. In my case, there was no doubt that something had changed. I knew I was new! I felt the release of tremendous tension and pressure on the inside, and peace, real peace, filled me like I'd never been filled before.

I hardly had time to appreciate what happened when Mike turned to me with a big smile on his face and said, "You know, there's more." Just that simply and directly, he went right on to tell me that now that I had become a Christian, I needed power to live the Christian life just as the disciples had needed it back in the beginning. I needed His power to live it so that I would be a witness, an example to others of what life in Jesus was all about.

He talked about something he called the baptism with the Holy Spirit. Then he showed me in the Bible how the early Christians had received it, what an effect it had on Peter, how it had transformed him from a man who knew Jesus but was afraid to admit it into a man who proclaimed Him before crowds on Pentecost, and three thousand were converted to the Lord. He read me the verse where Jesus Himself said, "You shall receive power when the Holy Spirit has come upon you; and you shall be My witnesses" (Acts 1:8).

I wanted all God had for me, and so for the second time in less than half an hour, I bowed my head and Mike led me in prayer. I experienced what hundreds and thousands of believers had experienced before me, that God in His great love wants not only to fill us to overflowing within, but also to clothe us with the power of His Holy Spirit, that we might be willing and able ambassadors to the world around us. Then we can let them know by our lives as well as by our words that Jesus is alive, that His love is without end and His mercies without number, that He is coming back again for His own, that His Word is true and will never fail, and that He alone is Savior, Messiah, Lord, and Christ.

Mike was as excited as I. Joy bubbled over in that '66 red Mustang. The power of God had touched my life, and I would never be the same again.

We got out of the car to take a closer look at the statue on the hill and to enjoy the beauty of our Father's creation that lovely summer evening. As I stood there reveling in the reality of Jesus Christ in a way I'd never known it before, Mike was standing a few feet away from me, calm and peaceful on the outside, but struggling within.

The Lord had begun to move upon him that he should baptize me in water in order that my salvation experience might be complete. He argued with the Lord, reminding Him that I was Catholic, and an ex-nun besides. He couldn't possibly baptize me; it would frighten me, turn me off, etc. I needed teaching about immersion, needed to get into the Word and learn, etc., etc., etc. All of his theological objections did not impress the Lord in the least; He continued to speak into Mike's spirit, "Baptize her."

After what seemed to him an interminable length of time, but was actually just a few minutes, Mike very cautiously and laboriously began explaining that part of being a Christian was learning to hear the voice of God and to be willing to obey even when it was difficult to understand what God was saying. On and on he talked until I wondered what he was getting at, for though I understood what he was saying, it seemed as though he was leading up to something.

Finally, he ventured that he felt that the Lord was telling him that I should be baptized in water. He wondered what I thought of that.

I paused for a moment, and only one thought crossed my mind. As an infant I had been baptized by someone else's choice and someone else's profession of faith. In view of the commitment I had just made, it seemed reasonable to me that I should be baptized by my own choice and to testify to my own voluntary commitment. No other thoughts came to me so I said, "I think that would be good."

As only the Lord could have planned it, at the foot of the hill was a small pond. We waded in up to our knees, and I was baptized. The presence of God touched me very deeply for the third time in less than an hour. The day of my salvation was truly an overwhelming experience. I was free, so free, really and truly free.

I rejoiced at my newfound life; Mike rejoiced at another soul being added to the kingdom; angels rejoiced in heaven.

Mike drove me home and dropped me off with a final encouragement to find a good Bible-preaching church where I would get fed the Word of God, and with an invitation to attend the prayer meeting with my roommate, Annette.

The grin on my face as I came through the door was all Annette needed to see. With a bear hug and a resounding "Praise the Lord!" she let me know she knew what had happened. We talked for quite a while, and much too late we decided we had better get some sleep.

As I went from the bedroom down the dimly lit hallway to the bathroom, sometime between 11:30 P.M. and midnight, suddenly a memory broke into my consciousness. A penetrating realization gripped me as I heard again in my mind the words I'd heard in the convent several weeks earlier: "The one who baptizes you will be the one I have chosen."

I froze for a few moments and then dashed into the bathroom, leaning heavily against the door as I closed it behind me.

"Oh, God, you've got to be kidding. He's a Protestant ...my mother will kill me...I don't know anything about him...he knows too much about me...oh, all those awful things I told him about myself this afternoon." On and on it went, thought after disjointed thought racing through my mind. I stayed in the bathroom so long Annette came knocking at the door to see if I was all right.

How much later it was I don't recall, but that very night, I made perhaps the second most important decision of my life. That God was real and that He still spoke today was indisputable. I believed that He had spoken to me. I was sure that He was able to bring to pass that which He had spoken. I was also convinced that He could do it most successfully without my interference.

I knelt down right there on the cold gray and pink tiles of that old bathroom and made a second commitment to the Lord that night, a commitment that was really the first fruit of the one I'd made several hours earlier—to surrender the lordship of my life to Jesus. I gave over to Him this man named Mike Richmond. I promised Him that I would say nothing and do nothing about what I believed He had said to me concerning this man. I would pray for him and do nothing more than what the natural course of events might bring my way. If it was indeed His will, I wanted with all my heart that it be accomplished in His way and in His time.

I wonder if my guardian angel smiled....

VIII

HEALING: DOES IT STILL HAPPEN?

One of the exciting things about becoming a Christian is not only developing a personal relationship with Jesus, but getting to know a whole new family. Brothers and sisters in the body of Christ are family indeed. As I became more and more a part of the prayer group, joy increased with shared fellowship. Having long lamented the lack of natural brothers and sisters, I now had more than I could count. It was delightful.

During my last year in the convent someone had donated a guitar which I had been given permission to tinker with. This first year after becoming a Christian I found myself more and more drawn to practicing and learning some of the inspiring and enthusiastic Scripture songs we sang in the meetings.

Alone in the apartment one afternoon, I was finishing up in the kitchen and planning to spend some time with my new guitar, one of my first purchases. Soft music from the living room attracted my attention. I thought it a bit strange since there was no radio in there, so I dried my hands to investigate. As I went into the living room, it stopped. I returned to my dishes, assuming the music had come from another apartment.

Moments later, I heard the same song again. For a second time, it stopped when I went into the living room. After the third time I began to suspect that the Lord might be trying to speak to me. Picking up my guitar, I went into the other room and prayed. Soon I heard again the same song, sung by a male voice and accompanied by a lone guitar. When it was finished, I picked up my guitar and found I could play the entire song through, remembering every word and using some chords I didn't previously know.

A few days later, summoning all my courage, I shared the song at the prayer meeting, and to my amazement watched as the Lord ministered life and grace through it to the body.

Before long, my notebook was filling up with songs given to me by the Holy Spirit in this way. Little by little I was learning to hear His voice, to forget my fears, and to share what He gave me.

Mike and I would see each other at the weekly meeting, but there was nothing more than a good brother-sister friendship between us.

The Lord had miraculously provided me with a green Volkswagen shortly after I learned to drive. It gave me the wonderful freedom of getting to all the prayer meetings I could handle with my teaching schedule, as well as to other Christian meetings of special interest.

In the fall of 1969 I began regularly attending Our Savior's Lutheran Church in Albany, many of whose members were charismatic and most enthusiastic about their faith. The pastor's preaching inspired and challenged me. In my first few months as a Christian I hungered for the Word and spent as much time as possible reading and studying it. Gradually the Holy Spirit Himself weaned me from wrong doctrines and understandings. As the truth of the Scriptures came to bear on one or another of the doctrines I had previously believed, I would put the doctrine aside in favor of the Word, and God would bless me with a tremendous freedom which I cherish to this day. No man and no denomination turned me away from my previous allegiance to Rome, but the Word of God itself convicted me and corrected me. For His grace I am so grateful.

My little car and I also made some weekend trips to visit my parents, who at this time were not really aware that I had left the Catholic church. They knew that I was involved in some kind of prayer group, which to them was highly suspect, and understandably so since they knew nothing about it. They still hadn't totally recovered from my departure from the convent. I was sure they couldn't handle my departure from Catholicism as well.

My mother's birthday is in February. I had a long holiday weekend for Lincoln's birthday so I planned a trip home. It was a beautifully sunny, but bitterly cold day as I drove the turnpike on the way down. The four-hour trip was pleasant, and I especially loved the drive through the Berkshires.

We had a good time shopping on Saturday. I accompanied them to Mass on Sunday, all the while missing the vibrant service I knew was taking place at Our Savior's. We celebrated Mom's day with a cake in the afternoon. I had decided to leave for Albany Monday at noon, planning to be back in my apartment by dinner time, get a good night's sleep, and be ready for school Tuesday morning.

Monday morning was gray and overcast, the kind of sky that tells a New Englander snow is in the air. Caution told me I should leave a little earlier rather than risk a storm later in the day. By 11:00 I was on the highway. Just a few miles west of Boston it started snowing, lightly at first, then more heavily. It was that wet snow, good for snowballs and giant snowmen that last for weeks, but terrible for driving. I was two hours into the trip, halfway home.

By mid-afternoon few cars were on the turnpike, and those who were crawled at a snail's pace on treacherous road conditions. The windshield wipers kept jamming up on the wet snow, and every few miles I stopped to clear the windows and wipers by hand.

As I approached the exit for Chicopee, Massachusetts, I considered pulling off to take a motel room for the night, thinking I could complete the trip more easily in the early morning. While deliberating over this, a tractor trailer passed me on the left, spraying dirty snow and ice all over my windshield. Still very much the inexperienced driver, I nervously pulled over once more to clean the covered windshield. Distracted, I went on and drove past the exit ramp in the storm without realizing it. I was now crawling at about twenty miles per hour.

It was 4:00 P.M., and under normal conditions I would have long since been home, warm and dry, but at the rate I was now traveling I was still at least two hours from that cozy apartment. I saw signs for Exit 2, Lee and Stockbridge, and knew I was nearing the New York state line.

The next thing I remember is the car sliding wildly

across the highway, out of control. I went around in a circle and slid into the concrete abutment along the median. The car flipped over once, twice, three times, while I cried out, "Jesus! Jesus! Jesus!" as I was being thrown around inside. It came to rest on its caved-in roof in the passing lane on the other side of the turnpike, in the path of an approaching tandem, hours behind his appointed schedule.

I sincerely believe that an unseen host of angels stopped that truck before it rode right over me and my little car. I was pinned and couldn't move. Footsteps crunched over the snow, and I heard a man's voice call out, "No one's alive in that one." I wanted to scream, "Oh, yes, I am," but the sound wouldn't come.

An ambulance appeared in record time. I was transported to the nearest hospital, carefully examined, and diagnosed as having massive tissue and ligament damage along my spine and neck. I was practically immobilized, then told that I would need prolonged bed rest and in all probability would not walk for many months.

I remained in that hospital for several days. The doctor then suggested that I be moved to Albany to be close to friends. He felt I could handle the hour's ride without undue stress. The necessary calls were made, and I waited somewhat impatiently for the coming Thursday's trip. I was eager to get back to Albany, to my praying friends, back where faith for healing was part of the spiritual atmosphere, back where I could be surrounded and encouraged by my brothers and sisters in the Lord.

I was transferred gently and carefully to the waiting vehicle, propped up comfortably and covered with a warm blanket. The bright sunshine made me squint as the mounds of snowbanks glistened in the rays. It was crisp and clear, not a wisp of a cloud anywhere in the blue skies. An occasional bump in the road reminded me all too well of the extensive injuries in my body, but otherwise the trip was uneventful.

I awoke with a start as the driver turned off the ignition. The short nap had brought me to the end of the trip, and I looked up to see three happy faces smiling their welcomes. Sally, Heather, and Pat, members of the prayer community, were waiting to greet me with messages, hugs, and flowers from many in the fellowship.

Love was so nice to come home to.

A few short hours later my joy turned to fear and then to panic as I began to hemorrhage. Medical personnel scurried about and soon determined that I had a lacerated left kidney which had not been detected. The stress of the trip precipitated the hemorrhaging, and my condition rapidly worsened. Various routine treatments were administered, but my body did not respond. Daily I grew weaker. The doctors were puzzled, and surgery was finally suggested.

Very late the evening before I was to be taken up for surgery the following morning, a small group of leaders gathered to intercede for me. One of them, a gentle, fatherly friend named Wylie Childs, came to the hospital to anoint me with oil and pray. Heavily sedated as I was, my memory of his coming is very blurred, but heaven knew...and listened.

The morning after surgery I awoke early, having been asleep for more than twenty-four hours. The institutional green walls and stark surroundings confused me as I groped to remember who and where I was. Piece by piece it came back to me. The accident...Exit 2...hemorrhage...surgery... ah, yes, surgery. Without thinking I moved my right arm under the stiff white sheet to feel for bandages. Then I moved my left arm. Then I lifted my head slightly off the pillows.

"Wait a minute," I exclaimed out loud. "Wait a minute. I haven't moved my arms without pain for two weeks. Oh, Lord...." I turned my head from side to side; I lifted one arm and then the other; still no pain. I tried to sit up and to my amazement, did so with no pain or stiffness. There were no bandages, no evidence of surgery whatsoever. For a fleeting moment I actually wondered if I were dreaming. A familiar hospital intercom call to "Dr. Smith, please, Dr. Smith" assured me that I was very much awake.

As the realization of the drastic change in my condition began to dawn on me, and my curiosity concerning the surgery, or lack of it, mounted, I reached across to the nurse's call button. Hesitating, I decided I would like to see whether or not I could stand. If I could, I would use the lavatory, then I would call the nurse.

At this point I had been confined to bed for well over two weeks, yet now I stood up and walked across the room, not only without pain, but also without any sensation of dizziness or weakness.

A young nurse walked past my door down the hall just in time to catch a glimpse of me as I walked back to the bed. Screaming, "Doctor! Doctor," she ran down the corridor, only to return in less than a minute with two doctors and three nurses all gazing at me in disbelief. At first they would not answer any of my rapidly fired questions, but instead examined and reexamined me, pulling, poking, pricking, and pushing. The most I could get from the resident was a non-committal, "We don't yet understand what has happened to you. As soon as we've arrived at a diagnosis, we'll talk with you." With that, he excused himself.

One young nurse lingered and asked me several questions, which even I was hard pressed to answer. But one thing I knew. I was whole again, and I knew who had done it. That much I could tell her: that Jesus healed me because of prayer. How I came to be whole I did not know, but I knew who had healed me. She listened quietly and blinked back a tear as she left the room.

Later that day I was released with a clean bill of health. X-rays had proven what I already knew. It was one of those experiences that doctors relegate to "conditions beyond our knowledge or control."

An operating room nurse later filled me in on some of the missing details. The previous morning I had indeed been taken up for surgery, but my condition had so deteriorated that a last minute decision was made to cancel the procedure. I was returned to my room and left with little hope of survival, one of those discomforting cases to a doctor, a patient who doesn't respond according to the textbook, whose body defies accepted medical treatment and doesn't tell the doctor why.

But God...God had a reason, a purpose, a plan. He healed me completely, and since that 25th of February, 1970, I have never again had any kind of problem with that left kidney. It functions normally. The muscles, ligaments and tissue in my back and neck are fine and healthy, and I, who was told to expect months of prolonged bed rest and therapy, was back in school teaching a full schedule in three weeks.

God never stopped dispensing His miraculous healing power. His arm, as the Scripture says, is not shortened, neither is His ear dull. He told His people Israel centuries ago, "I am the Lord that healeth thee." It is we in the church who stopped believing Him for too many years. The Word rings true today, and it has through the ages, that He is our Lord who heals us.

IX

What God Hath Joined Together

Pentecost Sunday, 1970. I arose early, anticipating the events of the day. My thoughts turned back to Pentecost a year ago when the Lord first told me that the man who would baptize me was His choice for my husband.

A year, I mused to myself. I reflected on how much had happened since then and wondered how God would yet work to fulfill His word to me. Over the last months, especially since God had healed me, Mike and I had become fast friends, closer than many natural brothers and sisters. We could talk about anything with each other, and when we prayed together it seemed as if all of heaven stopped to listen. Several times when Mike had been invited to speak at some Christian meeting or in a church service, he had asked me to accompany him to share a portion of my testimony or to minister in music. It was a beautiful relationship, and we had wonderful times together in the Lord, but romantic it was not. There was nothing about it that looked like a marriage was in the future.

We had spent many hours working with other leaders in the area planning this grand Pentecost celebration. Christians of all denominations were joining for the day in worship, fellowship, and a "family" picnic.

I heard the toot of a familiar horn, grabbed my guitar and the picnic lunch I'd prepared for the two of us, and hurried out the door. Mike greeted me with a cheery "Happy Pentecost" and a quick hug as he relieved me of the guitar and lunch basket and promptly deposited them in the trunk.

By the time we arrived, several rows of cars were already parked outside the high school where the all-day meeting was to be held. The Reverend John Bertolucci, the main speaker for the day and a man brand new to the renewal movement at that time, greeted us warmly as we entered the auditorium, then went off with Mike and the other men to pray before the opening service. I took my place with the other musicians, busily tuning their instruments.

The worship was exuberant, the prophetic word flowed like honey, and Father John's message was dynamic. Probably few of us realized then the extent to which God would use him in the years ahead, but how we enjoyed his ministry among us in those days when he was part of the local Christian community in the Albany area.

Driving home that evening, tired but exhilarated, Mike and I discussed some of the beautiful things God had done during the day. Over a quiet cup of tea our conversation turned more personal. Mike turned to me with a silly grin playing on his face and said, “Barb, the Lord told me something that startled me today, but it’s really true and I need to tell you. He told me that I needed to face the fact that I’m really dating you.”

He stopped and looked for my reaction.

With all kinds of bells and whistles going off inside of me, I managed to smile and say, “Oh, really?”

“We’ve been blessed with such a tremendous friendship,” he continued, “and we’ve become so close that I just haven’t named it for what it is.” And with his warm smile, he concluded with a flourish of his hand. “So, there, now it’s out; we’re dating! What do you think of that?”

We both laughed about it, finished our tea, then spent a little time praying before he left for home.

I prayed a long time before I went to sleep that night. I prayed for Mike, whom I already loved very deeply. He had lost his mother when he was six and his father when he was eight. Raised by elderly grandparents who loved him but were without the energy and stamina to invest the time and personal attention he and his brother and sister needed, Mike had pretty much raised himself. Discipline was almost nonexistent. He was sent to church but never taken there. It was not a close family, and when he was confirmed in the Lutheran church, no one came to the service. When Mike graduated from junior high school, no one in the family was there. When he left home to enter the Coast Guard at age eighteen, his sister and cousin drove him to the station and dropped him off, not even waiting until the train pulled away.

Mike had learned early to work and take care of himself because no one else would. And he’d told me once how he’d felt lonely as long as he could remember. I’d noticed tears in his eyes as he spoke. He was never really sure anybody cared until he met Jesus in a very real way.

The Lord had His hand on Mike's life for a long time. At ten years of age he signed his name in the back of a Gideon New Testament, praying alone to receive the Lord into his life. No one told him then "that with the heart man believes unto righteousness," as it says in Romans 10, "but with the mouth confession is made unto salvation." He had received the Lord but had no fellowship and no teaching to bring him into the fullness of what the Lord had for him and to teach him how to live in the kingdom of God.

So he continued through the years, very lonely, wanting God and not quite knowing what to do beyond Sunday church attendance and reading the Word, which his Lutheran background had taught him to do.

In July 1966, at the age of twenty-seven, life really began for him. Through a young people's prayer group he recommitted his life to Jesus as not only Savior, but Lord as well, and was filled with the Holy Spirit in a new dimension. He glowed when he told me how his life had changed, how real Jesus had become to him, how the Bible came alive, and how he wanted nothing more than to serve the Lord faithfully.

Once we had talked of marriage—not our marriage, but marriage in general. He prayed for a wife, longed to be married yet battled a very real fear. Every marriage in his family was unhappy; many had ended in divorce. He had seen firsthand the wrenching pain of broken relationships and hurting children. He had prayed, he told me, that God would protect him from that kind of experience. As much as he desired a family, he told the Lord with tears in his eyes that he would rather remain single all of his life than to live through the kind of pain he'd seen — or even worse, to watch any of his own children suffer in that way.

We had prayed together then for each other, he not

knowing what the Lord had told me. I had come away from him that night, as I did again this night, overwhelmed at the tremendous lack of love in his early life, while I had been so blessed with a secure home and parents who were always there for every event.

I prayed for Mike, but I prayed for myself as well. I cried out to God to make me the kind of wife Mike needed and God wanted. I marveled at the grace of God in this man I loved, for he was, and is, a sensitive and compassionate person, the kind of man sought out by those who are hurting. I saw that he had become not a victim of his past, but a product. He had somehow learned from the Holy Spirit the secret of turning pain into promise, hurt into health, and fear into faith.

He believed God.

We were engaged on August 27, 1970, after God spoke clearly to him, "This is the one I have chosen for you; marry her." From a foundation of a strong and healthy friendship grew the kind of love that makes a marriage.

The Christian community turned out in record numbers on October 24 for our wedding. About one hundred invitations had been mailed, but as the organ played "All Hail the Power of Jesus' Name" and I walked down the aisle to Mike, more than five hundred believers sang and rejoiced with us.

Father Bertolucci was the master of ceremonies for the wedding service and led the worship until the old cathedral rang with the praises of God. Seven priests and ministers, all leaders in the various segments of the Christian community in that area and all friends of ours, participated in the service held in a Catholic church out of deference to my family. Friends and relatives came from distant places to attend a wedding, but went home, according to their own testimonies, transformed by the power of God.

The congregation sang the words of the old hymn with electric enthusiasm, and as we walked down the aisle, arm in arm, in my heart I echoed the words they were singing as I looked up and smiled at *my* husband, "To God be the glory, great things He has done."

And someplace in the crowd, Mrs. Nattelle beamed and wiped away a tear as she thought about a little paperback she gave me on a quiet afternoon in the fall, just about two years before. Under no conditions would she have missed being present at this wedding.

X

First Fruits Unto God

"It's a girl!" My mother squealed at the other end of the phone. She had been hoping for a granddaughter since that day several months earlier when we had announced to her that we were expecting a child. Mike and I kept talking about a boy, but here *she* was, a bouncing seven pound, nine ounce baby girl with plenty of dark hair and a round face.

Elizabeth Michelle was born on January 16, 1972, four weeks earlier than her projected due date, but obviously full term and right on time. There had been some confusion as to the exact time that the baby was due, and in early December Dr. Jorgensen greeted me with the announcement that she suspected I was having twins. My uterus was too large for one seven month fetus, and she thought she had detected two heartbeats. She was so certain of a multiple birth, in fact, that she issued an insurance form to that effect to be submitted ahead of time to the agent.

On Sunday, January 9, the women of Our Savior's Church had surprised me with a lovely baby shower—for twins! Everything was yellow, and everything was doubled! We laughed and chattered over the possibilities of two boys, or will it be two girls, or one of each? And what will you name it, I mean, them? It was a beautiful shower, and I went home abundantly laden with more than enough for two precious babies.

The very next Sunday Elizabeth made her grand entrance into the world...alone! I was convinced the poor child would grow up despising the color yellow. It's all she wore for the first few months, except for the two or three pink outfits purchased by the proud new grandmother. A baby girl just had to have pink!

She was indeed a blessing from the Lord, and as a new mother I thought I could not be happier. She was such a good baby; she nursed well, slept well, and smiled easily. We had named her Elizabeth, and we called her Elizabeth. We still do. There may be an occasional Beth at school, but at home she's always our Elizabeth.

By the following September, I realized that our next child was on the way. Perhaps this time we would have our boy, our John Michael. Mike had always loved that name and for years had looked forward to giving it to his first son.

The pregnancy went well, and since Elizabeth was such a good baby, it was not difficult for me to care for her as well as get the rest I needed as the months went on. The baby was due on April 27, Mike's birthday. I fervently prayed that a son would be his birthday gift. All the arrangements for Elizabeth's care were made well in advance, and I was so sure of having a son that I packed a pale blue outfit to bring him home from the hospital.

On April 4 I awoke not feeling well, and by mid-afternoon I was experiencing labor pains. The doctor was consulted and advised complete bed rest. It was three weeks too early, and she was concerned. At my last checkup Dr. Jorgensen had commented that this baby would not be as large as Elizabeth had been, for it was still quite small.

The next two days and nights dragged by slowly with my having irregular but steadily stronger contractions. By the evening of April 6, I was admitted to the hospital and was being treated in an attempt to stop the progress of labor. It was too late.

Before 6:00 A.M. the following morning, John Michael Richmond was born, weighing in at just five pounds. It was a long and difficult labor and a breech birth. He was born exhausted, and from the first moments we knew something was wrong. The doctor laid him on my stomach momentarily, and the tiny body was still and silent. A nurse picked him up quickly and whisked him away to the far corner of the room, working desperately to get him to breathe. After what seemed an interminable amount of time, Mike, who was standing close to me at the head of the delivery table, heard a weak cry. He leaned over and whispered in my ear, "He just cried."

Totally exhausted and almost delirious, I couldn't think clearly. I wanted to see him, but they told me he wasn't ready. I could see him after he was washed, they said. Mike realized far more than I did at that point — that they were delaying telling me the truth.

While the nurses prepared me to return to the room, Mike went to the phone and called one of our best friends, Fritz. It was about 6:30 A.M. and Fritz, with his wife, Sylvia, would be getting ready to attend a breakfast meeting of the Full Gospel Businessmen's Fellowship that morning. Fritz was the vice president of the Albany chapter and usually helped run the meetings with Mike, who was chapter president that year.

"Fritz, Mike here. I'm at the hospital; Barb just delivered a boy. Fritz, we need a miracle. He's not well...can't breathe...premature. Please take over the meeting this morning and have the people pray. I've got to get back to Barbara. Thanks a lot, Fritz."

Over five hundred believers were in attendance at the breakfast that morning, and when Fritz announced the birth of John Michael Richmond, there was a ripple of spontaneous applause. He raised his hand to interrupt it, and the look on his face alerted the audience to the need for prayer. As he shared the problem, those Christians rose as one man, we are told, and went to their knees in that large banquet room to intercede for the life of a tiny boy, struggling for breath in a hospital less than three miles away. They prayed and cried out to God for his healing, many of those praying there remembering how they had cried out to the Lord just three years earlier for that baby's mother, and how God had raised her up miraculously.

Their faith was strong, their prayers prolonged. Many wept.

As soon as the meeting was over, John Bertolucci, Wylie Childs, and others came directly to the hospital to pray. They were allowed into the nursery with Mike where John Michael was being carefully monitored. Father Bertolucci wept openly as the saw that tiny frame with a head full of dark curly hair just like his daddy's.

At 4:30 that afternoon he died.

We wept for a long time and prayed through our tears.

I was in shock. I — who had been so amazingly healed

by the power of God, who believed wholeheartedly in His healing grace, in the anointing of oil by the laying on of hands, who told others about it — I laid in that bed brokenhearted, unable to say anything but, "Jesus, Jesus, Jesus."

How we had longed for that son; how many years his very name had been on Mike's heart; how much physical suffering I had endured in the last three days to bring him to birth.

And now he was gone.

It was a pain I had never known before; a pain unlike any other. There is a relationship that grows between mother and child even before birth. With every kick and movement, something is happening deep down that climaxes in birth, then continues to grow from there. I felt as though a part of me had died. In a way it did.

I still cry every April 7, but I thank God, too. There is a dynamic about pain and suffering that produces a fruit in us that nothing else can produce if we will receive from His hand and embrace situations and difficulties such as John Michael's death. We sometimes forget how well the Father understands us. He can comfort us, He can soothe our broken hearts, and He can also lift us up and take us on with Him because after all, He was in the same place when our son died that He was when His Son died. He was on the Throne, victorious, glorious, and looking with love from the other side of death. John Michael is rejoicing in His presence, and we haven't really lost him because we know right where he is. We see him as our first fruits unto God, and there is coming a day when we shall again be united around the throne of Him who rules and reigns forever.

And I still believe in the power of God to heal, in the anointing oil and the laying on of hands. I still tell others about it, pray with some, and see them healed just as I was.

Do we understand all about John Michael? Oh, no, but one thing we do understand. The Word of God is true and eternal. It never fails. And Jesus is Lord—in all, of all, and over all.

No, we don't understand everything, but it is enough for us that He understands. He is Lord. We can trust Him implicitly.

XI

We Go On

"Until He Comes" was the title of the sermon listed on the bulletin that morning. It was a well-prepared message to be sure and eloquently delivered, but I don't remember a word of it. All that day and through the week, those three words burned over and over in my heart: "Until He comes…until He comes…."

It was August of 1975. Mike and I and our two little girls had just returned from a summer of missionary service in the Azores Islands, seven hundred miles off the coast of Portugal.

The summer after John Michael's death, God had graciously opened the opportunity for Mike to attend Elim

Bible Institute in Lima, New York, to pursue full-time study of the ministry. During his freshman year God had blessed us with our second beautiful daughter, Susan Melissa, born in 1974. Susie was every bit a delight with a sweet disposition, sparkling hazel eyes like her daddy's, and a constant smile. She won everybody's heart on the island of Terceira that summer. Her light hair was a mass of curls, and at a year and a half, she was a charmer. She and Elizabeth had weathered the trip nicely, and we had been challenged with the opportunity to be involved in grass roots evangelism.

The summer of service on an island with little electricity, even less plumbing, and extremely poor people brought home to us the spiritual poverty of a world without Jesus Christ far more vividly than any textbook or missions magazine could. It taught us very convincingly the insignificance of material possessions and earthly pursuits compared to the eternal value of leading one person into the kingdom of God and everlasting life. There was nothing else worthwhile to do but serve Him with all our heart and lives—until He comes.

Mike's senior year passed quickly, and just a few short weeks before graduation, the Father blessed us with a son. This time we got to keep him. Victor Edward was born on April 19, 1976, with blonde hair (our only one!) and looking very much like his cousin, Mark, who was Mike's brother's boy who had perished in a house fire shortly after we were first married.

Victor was premature and developed breathing problems at birth just like his older brother. When just a few hours old he was transferred by ambulance to the Intensive Care Nursery at Rochester General Hospital. The tension we felt during those first few days was indescribable as all the memories of John Michael flooded our conscious thoughts. At times like those, praise is the greatest cure to troubled minds and spirits. Each time we felt beleaguered with negative pressure and fear, we chose with our wills to turn our attention to Him in praise and worship. Peace that didn't make any sense, if you will, the peace that passes understanding as the Scripture calls it, gently encouraged and stabilized us.

Mike and I made the twenty-five mile trip back and forth to the hospital every other day as Victor struggled to hold his own. Gradually he began to gain strength. After six long weeks and hundreds of hours of prayer on his behalf by so many at Elim and other places, Victor came home, weighing four pounds, fourteen ounces, fragile and tiny but having conquered the battle of those weeks by the grace and healing power of God. The Jewish neonatologist, the resident specialist in charge of the Intensive Care Unit, commented on the appropriateness of his given name, Victor. We prayed then, as we continue to do now, that his name will be prophetic and that he, along with his brother and sisters, will grow up walking before the Lord Jesus more than conquerors through Him who loves them.

Victor's homecoming was on the Friday morning inaugurating commencement weekend at Elim Bible Institute for the class of '76, a very special graduation for many reasons.

Mike had dreamed of Bible school training early in his Christian experience but had relegated it to the realm of the impossible. He was too old, had family responsibilities, a job, etc. But God had made his impossible dream come true.

And as if that weren't enough, on graduation morning his brother, his sister, and his aunt arrived after a five-hour drive for the commencement exercises. They heard him deliver the student address in the name of his class and saw him receive his diploma.

We had three beautiful children and a ministry opening up before us.

Great is His faithfulness!

In August 1978, after two happy years pastoring the Full Gospel Community Church in Warsaw, New York, we moved to a pastorate in southeastern Massachusetts near where I had been born and raised. Shortly afterward, our last child was born. Stephen Paul was named for the first martyr in the early church and for a dearly loved friend and brother in the Lord, the Reverend Paul Johansson, who with his wife, Gloria, have blessed and enriched our lives beyond the telling.

Our lives were full and exciting, but not nearly as exciting as the reunion we were about to experience!

XII

Whose Daughter?

Thanksgiving Day, 1978. I rose early to nurse two-month-old Stephen and enjoy quiet fellowship with the Lord at the same time. The darkness of night was just making way for the gray tints of pre-dawn as I settled myself comfortably on the sofa with Bible and baby.

There is something special, something unique about early morning hours with the Lord. Just as Israel gathered manna for the day in the early hours before dawn, there is a gathering into our lives of the manner of strength, of intimacy, of power, of grace, and of wisdom that comes on the wings of the morning hours when we give them as first fruits of our day unto Him.

"In the morning you hear my voice, O Lord; in the morning I prepare [a prayer, a sacrifice] for You, and watch and wait [for You to speak to my heart]" (Psalm 5:3, Amplified Bible).

It was one of those mornings. His presence came softly like a tender embrace, and I prayed peacefully as Stephen nursed. Then He spoke to me.

"Your mother is alive. I want you to find her."

I sat stunned and still. First one tear and then another trickled slowly down my cheeks.

I knew that Voice. He'd spoken to me before, and He'd been right — so right, so long ago in that convent chapel.

The realization of what He'd said began to take hold of me, and my crying turned to laughter, bubbling up from deep within.

Mike got up as I was tucking the now sleeping Stephen back into his crib. He leaned lovingly over my shoulder to gaze affectionately at our youngest son. With one hand he tilted my head up to his for a good morning kiss and noticed my tear-stained face.

"Honey, what's wrong?"

For as long as he'd know me, Mike had known my thoughts and wonderings concerning my real parents. As I shared with him what God had spoken to me, he knew so well what I was feeling.

We prayed together and committed it to Jesus from whom it had come. Wisely my husband decided we should let the matter sit for a while and seek the Lord's specific directions before we began to search for Norma Cleaves. How often we abort the purposes of God when He wants to move in a specific area by running off way ahead of Him. We hear what He wants to do, and like an enthusiastic child, we begin to run with *what* we've heard He wants, but don't wait for His instructions on *how* or *when* He wants it done.

I thank God for a husband who has learned this lesson.

Three weeks and some days later — three weeks that seemed more like three years to me — on a cold, bright morning in December, we drove the twelve miles to Fall River and made our way into the offices of St. Anne's Hospital where I had been born. As we expected, medical files are confidential. Norma Cleaves' signature authorizing release was required to obtain any information concerning her or newborn baby Cleaves.

However, just inquiring about the records brought some very helpful advice. If we would like to go to City Hall, the clerk there would make available the city records for the year in which I had been born, and by matching names, we would locate addresses, perhaps other family members still living in Fall River. It was suggested that we even follow the name through succeeding years to see if there might be a record of said Norma Cleaves being married and to whom. It was a good place to start, so we thanked our benefactor and turned to leave the hospital.

Passing through the lobby, I went over to the phone book just to flip through and see if perchance there were still any Cleaves families listed. As I scanned the pages and located three, my heart skipped. Two seemed to be numbers and addresses where these families resided, but there was a third, a Cleaves Vacuum Cleaner service.

Hmmm, I wondered. Mike suggested I give it a call.

"Cleaves Vacuum Cleaners. May I help you?" The voice was male and sounded busy. I could hear talking in the background.

"I'm visiting from out of town and…um…I'm trying to locate a Norma Cleaves. Would you know her by any chance?"

My throat was dry, my hands ice cold.

The answer was quick and clipped. "Yes, I know her,

but I won't give you any information."

My first positive ray of hope. I rushed on.

"But, please, I just want to know where she is...."

"I'm sorry, I won't give you any information. Now if you don't mind, I'm quite busy." The phone clicked. I tried to analyze what just happened. I wasn't quite sure what it meant, but I was excited. He may put me off on the phone, I thought, but now that I have a clue, I'm not quitting.

Mike reminded me that we needed to get to City Hall before the lunch hour traffic downtown. He also comforted me with the suggestion that the man on the phone, whoever he was, was perfectly within sound reasoning to withhold information from a total stranger.

The city clerk at the desk was very sympathetic and most helpful. We quickly located a Cleaves family, a large one at that, living on School Street in Fall River in 1945. The father, Mark B. Cleaves, was listed as the operator of a vacuum cleaning establishment. Several sons and daughters lived at the same address, one of them Norma, another Maurice, presently listed in the current files as the proprietor of the same business owned by the older Mr. Cleaves back in 1945. Could it be that I had just spoken to my Uncle Maurice on the phone? Or was it an employee of his? But he'd said he knew Norma. The thoughts scrambled through my mind in a disorderly fashion.

What next? I looked to Mike for direction and encouragement.

The vacuum cleaner shop was easy to find. As we parked, a friendly looking gentleman was helping an older lady lift a vacuum cleaner into her car. I sat and watched.

"Shall we go in?" Mike's question interrupted my thoughts.

There were two customers waiting to speak to the man behind the counter. We busied ourselves with "shopping" for a vacuum cleaner while we waited for the store to empty. I noticed an older gentleman working at a bench in the rear of the shop. Another uncle? Probably not, I reasoned. Don't get carried away, I scolded myself.

"What can I do for you?" The question was addressed to Mike. I held back, wanting him to do the talking now that the moment had arrived. As he began explaining our purpose in being there, he took from my trembling hands the original adoption papers, the legal documents that proved my original identity as Barbara Cleaves.

The man behind the counter looked at them and called over his shoulder to the other man working in the back.

"Bernie, come here." Showing him the papers, he announced to him, "This girl here is Norma's daughter. Did you know anything about that?"

The shocked look on the other man's face told us he didn't.

"He's your uncle, too," Maurice Cleaves went on to explain, as much to himself as to me. "You see, we were in the war in '45 overseas; never came back til '46. Must be Norma had you while we were gone, and by the time we got home they decided there was no use tellin' us. It was all over then. Well, I'll be…." His voice trailed off.

"No denyin' it," my Uncle Bernie offered. "She looks just like her. Looks a mite like Judy, too, don't you think, Maury?"

"Yeah, we know Judy." He turned back to me as he said this.

"You know about Judy?" He searched my face. As I nodded, he continued. "We had a lot of fun with Judy as she was growin' up, but we don't see her much anymore. Lives in Maryland now, I think, and her husband don't go much for family visitin'. Hard on Norma, you know. Last time she was home was for Mom and Dad's fiftieth wedding anniversary just a few years ago. My, that was a time. Too bad you weren't around for that; whole family was here from all over."

"Your grandpa's still alive." Now it was Uncle Bernie's turn to fill me in on more of the family history. As they talked I could see a certain excitement and interest growing; the reality of a new niece they'd never met was beginning to dawn on them.

"Yeah, he's in a nursin' home near where Norma lives. He doesn't remember much anymore — hardening of the arteries, you know — but you'll be able to see him. Boy, I wish you could've known Nana. She was a peach." He said it with real emphasis. It was plain to see that Bernie had loved his mother a great deal.

I was beginning to relax and enjoy this first encounter with blood relatives, but I was a bit impatient to get back to the subject of Norma.

"My mother, can you tell me where she is?"

"Well, as a matter of fact, she just left yesterday for California for the holidays; went to see our sister, Mary. She's married now — your mother, I mean — nice guy, very good to her. Anyway, she's in California for a couple of weeks. Tell you what I'll do. Let me call her as soon as she gets back and break the news to her. I'm sure she'll want to see you; I'm *sure* of that. But it'll be quite a shock after all these years. Let me call her and give her your name and address. She'll be back on the fourth."

I handed him the family snapshot I'd brought with me. "If you see her before I do, will you give her this? I want her to see her grandchildren."

"Handsome bunch of kids you got!" He smiled broadly and nodded. "Sure thing. Keep in touch now, will ya? I'll call her as soon as she gets home."

We left then, and two bewildered and surprised uncles

went home to tell the family about this niece who just turned up in the shop today. And would you believe that Norma never told us?

It snowed all day on January 4, hard! I kept looking out the window wondering if the planes were flying, if she really was getting home today. What time would he call her? Would she call me tonight? What would she say? What would I say?

It was a very long day.

XIII

Picking Up Where We Never Left Off

How does an artist describe a tree to a blind man? How do you convey the impact of being healed to someone who has never faced death? How do you explain what happens on the inside when a stranger, and yet not a stranger, walks through your door with a quivering smile, tears in her eyes, and thirty-four years of pent up emotion and disappointment bubbling to the surface?

We both cried; Mike cried. At first all we could do was look at one another, she staring almost unbelievably at the strong resemblance between me and her in her younger years, while I just gazed, trying to take in the reality that this very woman was *the* one I'd prayed for and wondered about all these years. Here she was…finally. It was January 7. My uncle kept his promise of contacting my mother as soon as she returned home. She had called me January 6 and made plans to come to my home the next day, only an hour's drive from where she lived.

We spent the day together, and as the hours ticked by, the threads of the story started coming together. She poured out to me her pain and disappointment, even her feelings of despair, on that day so long ago when she'd walked out of that hospital leaving me behind; how several times that day she'd wanted to run back and claim me; how, as she got older and better established, she'd wished there was a way to recover her lost child. She talked about Judy, about Nana and Grandpa, and about her husband, my stepfather.

Then it would be my turn for a while. As I talked she kept looking at baby Stephen, or one of the other children, as if wanting to look long enough to make up for lost time. Over and over she would say, "Four beautiful grandchildren—wow! Wait until Clint sees them. He'll go crazy!" Grandpa Clint, as my children would call him, just loved children, and our children love him.

A few days later, Mike and I and the children drove the forty-five minutes down the Cape highway to Marstons Mills, a quaint and picturesque Cape Cod town where the Perry homestead is located. My mother was waiting at the door as Mike swung the station wagon into the driveway. Overjoyed to see us again so soon, she ushered us into the warm kitchen, just as Clint came through the door from the living room.

He stopped short and stared at me open-mouthed. "My God, you look just like your mother!" With a hearty laugh and a warm hug I knew he welcomed me into his home, his family and his heart. Before long, little Richmonds were climbing up on Grandpa Clint's lap, and he was thoroughly enjoying their antics. He and Mike talked as though they'd known one another for years, while my mother and I giggled like school girls as we continued to discover more and more ways in which we are very much alike.

Within a couple of days, we shared with my adopted mother the news that we had met and visited Norma Cleaves. I thank God for her reaction. Though there was an emotional response of fear at first, she soon saw our continued love and care for her, our consistent attention to her and to her place as mother and grandmother in our family. She could then rejoice with me that the opportunity had come for answers to many of my wonderings and questions. Within a few weeks both mothers met and embraced, becoming one family with us. It has been a beautiful relationship ever since.

Through it all, the Lord was busy about many things. There was healing for me, no doubt. There were certain emotional pressures that had become a part of me and a part of my thinking patterns that found release and a place of freedom through meeting and getting to know my natural mother. I doubt this would have happened any other way. There were things I did not realize were even there, but my new freedom within shed light on what had been and now was gone.

My mother, too, experienced the healing touch of the Holy Spirit, setting her free from those deep-seated hurts that had been buried for years. She discovered through our relationship a new awareness of God and the Lord Jesus Christ. She recognized that it was He who brought us together and oh, how grateful I was for that.

And I believe my adopted mother was touched with a different kind of healing power; the healing of being able to recognize that her inability to bear her own child had been not a curse from God, but a means of blessing; that He had taken that very problem which was so devastating to her and turned it into a vehicle of blessing that not only enriched her life and mine, but also became a source of great joy and comfort to my natural mother when we all finally came together.

Only the Lord can bless and bless and bless...so many...in so many ways...and all at the same time.

XIV

Coming Full Circle

"Fasten your seat belts, please. We're ready for takeoff" I settled into my seat by the window trying to contain my excitement. A lifetime dream was about to come true: Mike and I were on our way to Israel for what would prove to be the first of many trips over the next few years.

From my earliest years I had a keen interest in the Holy Land and its people. Jewish music evoked strong feelings in me and when, as a sophomore in high school, I read *The Diary of Anne Frank* I wept for days.

This was the land of the Bible, and the Jews were its people. At times, I wished I could have been alive when Jesus walked the hills and roads of Galilee. But many other Christians I knew who loved the Lord deeply did not seem to have such a love for the land of Israel. I wondered why I did.

It was only after the reunion with my birth mother that I truly understood. My father, who was killed in action on the battlefields of France two months before I was born, had been a Jew. His parents had joined the Catholic Church during World War I in order to protect the family by hiding their Jewish heritage. As the world neared the outbreak of World War II and news reports began to trickle out regarding the fate of Jews in Eastern Europe, the Rafael family withdrew even more from acknowledging their identity. They lived as an exemplary Roman Catholic family. But in a remote corner of their basement in a locked trunk, my grandfather carefully stored a pair of Shabbat candlesticks, a small menorah (the seven branched candelabra), thereadbare tallith (or prayer shawl) his father had passed down to him many years before, and an old mezuzah that had been a family treasure for three generations.

After my parents were engaged and just before my dad left for France, he took my mother down into the basement of his home and shared the family secret with her. I will be forever grateful that he chose to do so because had he not, I might never have known the truth. I might never have understood my love for things Jewish.

Several years later, through a series of God-ordained circumstances, Mike and I were finally on our way to Israel. It is difficult to express the depth of the impact the trip had on me.

I had already been a Bible teacher for some years, but as we stood atop Mount Carmel remembering Elijah's confrontation with the prophets of Baal; as we watched the sun come up over the Sea of Galilee; as we walked the streets of Old Jerusalem; as we climbed the Mount of Olives; the Scriptures came alive to me as never before. Passing through the Zion Gate one afternoon; Mike commented to me, "A trip like this should be a requirement for everyone in Bible college or seminary." Then he added thoughtfully, "Every Christian should come here at least once in his or her life." I heartily agreed. The spiritual impact is powerful. We decided then that leading Bible study trips to Israel at least once a year would become a major focus of our ministry.

In addition to the spiritual impact it brought, my time in Israel called to the forefront of my consciousness every bit of "Jewishness" in me. I felt completely at home, more comfortable and more contented in Israel than in any other place I'd ever lived. The tremendous inner healing I had experienced in the reunion with my birth mother came to its ultimate fulfillment in my visit to Israel. It was the closest thing I could experience to a reunion with my natural father, for whom I had felt a strong, seemingly unexplainable love. Perhaps in part it was because of some of the things my mother had said about him.— that he was kind, caring and full of life. But most of all, I remembered her saying, "You look so much like me in a lot of ways, Barbara, but you have your Daddy's smile, the smile that first stole my heart. After so many years, the memory of that smile still brought tears to her eyes. I thought of her words so many times as we made our way through Israel. I would look at people around me, especially the older men who were about the age my Dad would have been, and I'd think of him. I wondered if he ever longed to go home to "Eretz Yisrael" and what it might have meant to him to know his only daughter was so happy to be there.

The trip was over much too soon. Wiping away tears as the jumbo jet lifted off Israeli soil for the trip back to the United States, I looked out the window to watch the coastline of my beloved Israel disappear from view and whispered, "*Le-itra-hoi*. I'll be back soon."

Upon my return I plunged into the study of the Jewish Roots of Christianity with unrestrained zeal. The resources were quite limited in 1992, but I read everything and anything I could get into my hands. When I began to realize how profound and drastic the "divorce" was that occurred in the fourth century between the Christian Church and the Jews, I was deeply grieved. As I continued to study, the Lord showed me what had happened. He made it so easy for me to understand.

Just as I had been born of a Jewish father but was separated at a very young age from my true heritage (my roots), so His Church, born in Jerusalem and thoroughly Jewish in its beginnings, was torn away from its roots by the decrees of the Emperor Constantine. The longer the separation continued, the more the Church lost of its original identity as the fulfillment of all that the Hebrew Law and the prophets had pointed to and longed for in the person of Yeshua Ha'Masiach, Jesus the Messiah, the very One who *is* the Glory of Israel. Had not Jesus said, "I have not come to destroy the Law but to fulfill it." (Matt. 5:17)? With respect to us, did not Paul explain in his letter to the Romans, "the righteous requirement of the Law is fulfilled in you who believe..." (Rom. 8:4)?

Over the weeks the vision clarified as I recognized the parable God had written with my own life. Israel is like my natural mother who for years suffered a deep sense of loneliness for the "child" she had borne. A few months after our reunion, my mother said to me, "There were times in my life when I was so dissatisfied and restless, though I appeared to have no reason to feel that way. I had a good job, a good income, and a nice home. Everything seemed to be going along so well, but an inner feeling I couldn't explain just wouldn't go away." She paused reflectively, then continued, "I realize now that I was searching for

God... but I was also longing for my little girl. I feel so different since you've come back into my life."

There is a restlessness, a certain yearning and divine dissatisfaction among the people of Israel that is evidence of their longing for their Messiah. But I also believe that they long for their "daughter" to come home — that virgin daughter of Jerusalem spoken of by Isaiah; the church of the Living God.

Simultaneously, the Church is also in need of healing and restoration. The Lord spoke of this to a dear Israeli friend of mine, Dominiquae Bierman, in these words, "The Church is like a beautiful rose that has been cut off from the garden and from its roots. It has survived for two days inside a vase of water. But on the third day it will die unless it is replanted and reconnected back to its roots."

My reunion with my birth mother brought great healing into my life. Likewise, as the Church rediscovers its roots, and its heritage and restoration takes place, we will see a dimension of healing flowing through the Church unlike anything we have hitherto experienced. I found myself praying increasingly, "Lord, hasten the healing work of family reconciliation." The answer came quietly to my spirit, "I am hastening it and I have called you to be a part of it. Teach My Church about their Jewish roots."

There are so many others more educated, more learned than I in this field. But as the doors slowly opened for this teaching, I stepped into what the Lord had called me to do. With each successive trip to Israel, the Lord blessed me with additional contacts, new friends who taught me more and more. Invitations for me to teach the Word and to minister in churches and conferences around the world continued, but I noticed that the frequency with which these invitations requested ministry on Jewish Roots of the faith and things pertaining to Israel rapidly increased. Before long, more than half of my speaking engagements were Israel-related and that trend continues.

In the summer of 1995 on my first ministry trip into Mexico, I visited a remote Indian village. The village people proudly led me up a steep and rocky path to their small church. It was a rather primitive structure with no real windows, just square holes cut out in the adobe walls, nestled in the trees at the foot of a mountain. A wide archway welcomed me into the building where a door should have been.

As I entered the little church, I saw to my amazement, a large flag of Israel prominently displayed across the front wall. The Pastor's wife, the only person who spoke English in the village, smiled broadly and said, "We love Israel. We pray for Israel all the time. Please tell us more about it."

Sitting motionless on crude stone benches in 90 degree heat, the villagers listened intently to every word I shared with them about that beautiful land called Israel so far away and yet so near and dear to their hearts. They wept as I described the Sea of Galilee and the Garden of Gethsemane, and they shouted for joy as I taught them about the Feasts of the Lord and how much those festivals have to say to the Christian of the twentieth century. They were fascinated by the Jewish wedding customs that portray the coming of the Lord Jesus for His bride in the last days. They were thrilled at the realization that what the prophets had written so long ago was literally being fulfilled in our time in modern Israel.

I have sat in simple mud homes in Africa and taught the Jewish roots of Christianity to barefoot Zambian women hungry to learn more about the Bible they love so much.

I have seen several hundred people in a church in Siberia applaud Israel and pray for the peace of Jerusalem with great fervor and uncompromising faith.

I have watched the startled looks of men and women give birth to tears of repentance as the revelation grips their hearts that anti-semitism is not just a historical fact confined to World War II Germany, but is a present reality within the Church, perhaps even in their very hearts.

I have had countless Christians around the world come to me after a service or conference and ask, "Where have I been all my life?" "Why haven't we learned this before?" They exclaim, "What an impact this teaching is having on my love for Jesus and my relationship to Him! What a difference when I read my Bible now!" Member by member the Church is being healed; the separation is coming to an end, and the "daughter" is coming home!

By no means is the teaching on Jewish Roots of Christianity intended to propel the follower of Jesus to become a religious Jew and follow Rabbinical Judaism. Rather, its purpose is to bring us day by day and congregation by congregation closer to the great purpose of God's heart as seen in Ephesians 2:11-15: Therefore remember your former state: you Gentiles by birth — called the Uncircumcised by those who merely because of an operation on their flesh are called the Circumcised — at that time had no Messiah. You were estranged from the national life of Israel. You were foreigners to the covenants embodying God's promise. You were in this world without hope and without God. But now you who were once afar off have been brought near through the shedding of Messiah's blood. For He Himself is our Shalom (Peace) — He has made us both one and has broken down the wall which divided us by destroying in His own body the enmity occasioned by the Torah (Law) with its commands set forth in the form of ordinances. This He did in order to create in Himself from the two groups one new man…"

There it is — high priority item on God's agenda:

creating in Himself from the two groups, Jew and Gentile, *one new man* How can this be unless there is a healing and reconciliation between the two groups? And how shall that reconciliation take place without repentance, humility and mutual acceptance?

For the last two thousand years, the Church has been as the elder brother in the parable of the prodigal son who was at his Father's house, working in His fields, tending His flocks, meanwhile, wayward brother has been virtually forgotten and ignored since the time he rejected his Father's expressed love. But as "the times of the Gentiles" spoken of in Scripture approach their culmination, the prodigal is stirring in the far-off country. There is a new move of the Holy Spirit among the Jewish people, and they are beginning to turn toward home, toward Father and His love. The Father has been eagerly waiting for this day, earnestly anticipating the homecoming.

As the church is awakened to the need for reconciliation with our Jewish Roots, it is incumbent upon the Gentile to avoid at all costs the sin of the elder brother as we see our Jewish brethren blessed and favored by God. "For the time to favor Zion has come" (Psalm 102:13). May there be no jealousy, no resentment of the Father's goodness in restoring His chosen people and the land He promised them, no self-righteous arrogance that says, "We've been serving Christ all these years. Where have you come from?" Rather, let there be that joyous rediscovery of family unity, an exuberant spirit of celebration that the Father's awesome love has prevailed, tearing down every dividing wall and healing every breach.

Since my first visit to Israel in December of 1992 I have traveled there almost twenty times. People ask me at times if I ever get tired of taking groups to Israel, if it ever gets old. My answer is always the same. I smile and say, no.

Inwardly I wonder how going home can ever get old. Going home is wonderful and that's exactly how I feel every time I land on Israeli soil.

Both of my adopted parents have gone to be with the Lord: my birth mother is now gone as well. Mike and I have been married twenty-seven years, and two of our four children are now married as well. We joined that elite group of individuals on the earth called grandparents with the birth in 1994 of Garrett Alan Williams, the first son of our eldest daughter and her husband, Gregg.

God has been immensely good to me, and for that I praise Him with all my heart. It's been somewhat of a strange road, this life of mine, but never have I been happier than I am now. I count it a great privilege to teach the Word of God around the world and in some small way impact lives for Jesus Christ, for Yeshua Ha'Masiach.

It is clear from the signs all around us that time is short and the return of Jesus is fast approaching. We are a chosen generation, uniquely blessed to be alive in the days that prophets dreamed of centuries ago.

In our lifetime, Israel became a nation again after centuries of non-existence.

In our lifetime, worldwide communication has been established, making some of the events prophesied in Daniel and Revelation possible and feasible.

In our lifetime, the regathering of the exiles has and continues to take place.

In our lifetime, the birth pangs of the earth's redemption are being felt as never before in the history of the world with very significant increases in earthquakes, famines, wars, and rumors of wars. Jesus Himself said that the generation that saw these things would not pass away until He came again.

Your life, dear reader, has probably been fairly different from mine, but we are traveling toward a common end. We shall each stand before the Throne of God to give account of ourselves on that great Day. You could look at someone like me and think, "A nun…a pastor's wife…and a preacher herself besides. She's got it made." Not so! For it doesn't depend on what I've been or what I am today. My eternal salvation depends on who He is and what He's done for me by shedding His blood for my redemption. It's the same with you.

If you've been touched in any way by this story, I'm glad. But I am far more concerned that your heart be touched by the love of God as you may have recognized it in operation in my life. For He loves you just as much as He loves me. You *can* know for certain that you'll be with Him for eternity, not because of lofty deeds or heroic works that you have done, but simply by believing on the Lord Jesus Christ and receiving Him as your Savior and your Lord. If you have never surrendered your life and heart to the Lord Jesus Christ, the Messiah of Israel and Redeemer of all nations, will you pray with me?

Heavenly Father, I recognize that You have made the way for me to come to You through the life, death and resurrection of Jesus Christ, your beloved Son. I recognize my need for a Savior, and before all the principalities and powers of heaven and earth, I invite you, Lord Jesus to come ill to my heart, be my Savior and my Lord. I surrender myself completely to You to love You with all my heart and to follow You all the days of my life. I give You my life, and I receive Yours in exchange. Cleanse me of my sins by Your precious blood and make me a brand new person in You. Thank you, Lord. I receive you by faith and embrace the truth of your Word as the only reliable guide for my life from this day forward. In Jesus name, Amen.

If you have prayed this prayer and meant it with all your heart, we'd like to hear from you. Please write to: Barbara Richmond, For Your Glory, Inc., P.O. Box 3152, Titusville, FL 32781. Our Email address is: ruth311@juno.com

Next year in Jerusalem....maybe the *New Jerusalem*!

Need a Speaker for your Conference or Retreat?

Call our office to schedule Barbara Richmond
for your next retreat, convention or conference.
Barbara is a popular speaker and Bible teacher
across the United States and overseas.
Please contact our office for more information.

Phone: (407) 383-9229
Fax: (407) 383-1336